DOES THIS BEACH
MAKE ME LOOK FAT?

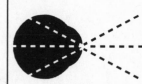

This Large Print Book carries the
Seal of Approval of N.A.V.H.

DOES THIS BEACH MAKE ME LOOK FAT?

LISA SCOTTOLINE
&
FRANCESCA SERRITELLA

THORNDIKE PRESS
A part of Gale, Cengage Learning

GALE
CENGAGE Learning

Farmington Hills, Mich • San Francisco • New York • Waterville, Maine
Meriden, Conn • Mason, Ohio • Chicago

GALE
CENGAGE Learning®

Copyright © 2015 by Smart Blonde.
All photographs courtesy of the authors except where indicated.
Thorndike Press, a part of Gale, Cengage Learning.

ALL RIGHTS RESERVED
Thorndike Press® Large Print Core.
The text of this Large Print edition is unabridged.
Other aspects of the book may vary from the original edition.
Set in 16 pt. Plantin.

LIBRARY OF CONGRESS CATALOGING-IN-PUBLICATION DATA

Scottoline, Lisa.
  Does this beach make me look fat? / by Lisa Scottoline & Francesca
Serritella.
    pages cm. — (Thorndike Press large print core)
  ISBN 978-1-4104-7734-7 (hardback) — ISBN 1-4104-7734-7 (hardcover)
  1. Women—Humor 2. Mothers and daughters—Humor. 3. Scottoline, Lisa.
4. Serritella, Francesca Scottoline. 5. Large type books. I. Serritella, Francesca
Scottoline. II. Title.
  PN6231.M68S3726 2015b
  818'.5402—dc23   2015017019

Published in 2015 by arrangement with St. Martin's Press, LLC

In loving memory of Mother Mary

CONTENTS

8

INTRODUCTION

BY LISA

People go to the beach for lots of reasons, namely, the sand, the sun, and the water.

I go for the food.

You might think there's no food at the beach, but if there's no food at your beach, come to mine.

Food never tastes better than it does on the beach.

How do I know this?

From a lifetime of eating on the beach.

You would think that the beach would be the last place you would eat, if you're a woman self-conscious about her body, which is every woman in the world.

But I grew up in a family of chubby Italian-Americans, and The Flying Scottolines didn't sweat the small stuff, especially the fact that none of us was what you would call small.

Mother Mary loved to cook, and the rest of us loved to eat, and none of us saw

11

anything wrong with it.

We had the time of our lives on the beach, because we were so full of food.

It's hard to be unhappy with a full tummy.

This was before the invention of Food Guilt.

Think back.

Because we Scottolines never had any Food Guilt.

Food is love, and we had a lot of love in our family.

We would *never* feel guilty because we ate.

We had guilt if we *didn't* eat.

And we had guilt about wasting food, which was our version of a mortal sin.

So before any trip to the beach, Mother Mary would cook up spaghetti and meatballs, so we could make spaghetti and meatball sandwiches to take to the beach. I know that not everybody has eaten spaghetti and meatball sandwiches, so here's the recipe:

To make a meatball sandwich, put a ton of meatballs in a hoagie roll and smash the top down. You can serve it hot or cold, but you should serve it on the beach.

Delicious.

The spaghetti sandwich is made the same way. Put a lot of spaghetti on a hoagie roll and smash the top down. It also works hot or cold and is perfect for the beach, because you'll spill so much tomato sauce on yourself that you'll have to go wash off in the water.

Not that I ever did that.

Less than two thousand times.

By the way, it goes without saying that you never put spaghetti and meatballs in the same sandwich.

Just in case you were thinking about it.

Don't embarrass yourself, or me.

And of course after we had our delicious meal on the beach, we'd be looking around for dessert, and in those days, an angel would appear in the form of the Ice Cream Man.

This wasn't a man driving an ice-cream truck like Mr. Softee, but a man who walked back and forth across the beach in the hot sun, wearing a white T-shirt and white long pants, lugging a massive cooler full of ice cream on his back.

Mr. Tuffee.

All the while he'd be calling out, "Ice cream and ices, ice cream and ices!" like a town crier for saturated fats.

And we would get our ice-cream treats, the first round of the day, but certainly not the last.

Because ice cream tastes better on the

beach, too.

There's nothing that doesn't taste better on the beach.

Mother Mary used to smoke on the beach, and she thought even cigarettes tasted better on the beach.

You can tell we weren't health nuts.

So then it won't surprise you that we couldn't swim.

Neither my mother, my brother Frank, nor I could swim at all. We never learned how, and to this day, we don't know.

Don't ask why.

The Flying Scottolines are full of mystery.

But my father could swim, and so for exercise we would go down to the water's edge and watch him, like three beach balls looking out to sea.

So given my altogether adorable childhood, it's hard to understand how I grew up and acquired Food Guilt, I-can't-believe-I-ate-that, a generalized fear of carbohydrates, and a lifelong worry about my weight. And I'm always on a diet, and I just now gained back the ten pounds that I had lost last month.

But more and more, especially in summertime when I'm sitting on the beach, I'm learning not to sweat it.

To go back to the child that I used to be.

To see myself through the loving eyes of my parents.

To eat on the beach.

And not to worry about whether every little thing makes me look fat.

In fact, not to worry *at all.*

And so that's very much the spirit of this book.

It's full of funny stories and true confessions from my daughter Francesca and me, and though we write about our bodies, we know that weight doesn't really have any weight with us.

It has to do with the stuff of life, yours and mine, as women in the world.

And at its warm little heart is a secret message:

Enjoy.

I'M NOT MY TYPE

BY FRANCESCA

I have a terrible personality.

According to Myers-Briggs.

My best friend sent me a version of the famous personality test to discover whether or not we would be good candidates for the CIA, hypothetically.

Because that's the type of idea my best friend and I come up with.

So she forwarded me a web link to a shortened version of the test.

Shockingly, neither of us had the spy personality; she was an INFJ and I came up with an INTJ. At first we were excited — we were just one letter off from each other — twinsies! It took a minute before I bothered to learn what my letters meant: Introverted, Intuitive, Thinking, and Judgmental.

"Is that good?" I asked her over Gchat, Google's instant messaging service.

"Yeah!" she typed. She was lucky I

17

couldn't see her face. "That's a very rare personality type."

She sent me an extended profile of my type. Sure enough, it said INTJs account for just 2% of the population, and female INTJs are only 0.8%.

I felt like a rare gem, a diamond.

Until I read the rest of the description. The only thing diamond-like about INTJ is a heart of coal.

The intro paragraph could be summed up as "Lady Macbeth."

"INTJs are defined by their tendency to move through life as if it were a giant chess board, always assessing new tactics, strategies, and contingency plans, constantly outmaneuvering their peers to maintain control."

Famous INTJs listed were Vladimir Putin, Lance Armstrong, Augustus Caesar (did you know Myers and Briggs lived Before Christ?), and Hannibal, among other Machiavellian rulers, egomaniacs, and cheats.

"I'm horrified!" I wrote to my friend.

"No! You could conquer the world!!!"

Three exclamation points are Internet-speak for overcompensating.

I can't possibly belong with these narcissists. Although, I do write about myself for

18

a living. And I'm a formidable Scrabble opponent. Does that count?

Another section speculated about fictional INTJs. The first was Walter White from *Breaking Bad.*

Okay, so the superfan in me loved this. At least it wasn't Lydia.

Also Gregory House from *House MD,* Hannibal Lecter from *Silence of the Lambs,* and Professor Moriarty, mortal enemy of Sherlock Holmes. Smart but heartless characters, ranging from a know-it-all misanthrope to a cannibalistic sociopath.

Put that in my OK Cupid profile.

The only decent one was Katniss Everdeen. I haven't read those books, but she's the good one in the kill-kids-for-sport game, right?

I'm not slinging arrows, I'm grasping at straws.

My friend's chat bubble popped up again: "You're right. This is so not you. Especially the parenting stuff."

Parenting section? I found it, and — *oof* — the INTJ parent makes the Tiger Mother sound like a kitten:

"Not prone to overt displays of physical affection . . . perfectionistic, often insensitive. When it comes to emotional support, INTJs . . . will likely never deliver the sort of warmth and coddling children crave."

I don't have children yet, but I have a dog and a cat who are my babies. I let them sleep in my bed, I kiss them on the mouth, I cook for them, and I tell them they are brilliant and beautiful — although they listen best when I'm holding a treat. I even brush my dog's teeth three times a week.

Believe me, I can coddle with the best of them.

I was Italian before I was INTJ.

At the end, the profile stated, "Remember, all types are equal."

Oh, sure. That's why you listed history's greatest super-villains in my group.

I hate this. My astrological sign, Aquarius, never suited me either. The descriptions say things like: a flighty air sign, a social butterfly, no one can hold on to you for long! Meanwhile, I've had the same five close girlfriends since I was eleven, I'm a serial monogamist, and I'm a homebody who enjoys nesting.

Aquarius wouldn't let me sit at her lunch table.

Anyone who has been on Facebook recently has seen their feeds inundated with those "Which Disney Princess/Dog Breed/ Game of Thrones House/Alcoholic Beverage Are YOU?" personality quizzes. Who among us hasn't clicked on one?

Who among us hasn't taken one twice for a better outcome?

The last one I took promised to tell me who would play me in a movie. My answer: Morgan Freeman.

I get that all the time.

I never believed in astrology, much less an online personality test, and yet I'm still curious and then disappointed when they aren't what I want to hear. What are we looking for in these quizzes? Validation? Recognition? Any excuse not to do work?

Well, I'm done. I'm more than a type, a star sign, or an algorithm. I know myself better than anyone.

And I'd be great in the CIA.

JUMPY

BY LISA

It's time you knew I had fleas.

As if I weren't single enough.

Apparently, being single is like being broke. You don't think you can get broker than broke, but you can.

Just ask the government.

Oh. Wait. They're closed.

Oh, sorry. They're open again.

Phew.

Anyway, it's not my fault I have fleas, it's my dogs' fault. As you may know, I have five dogs: Ruby The Crazy Corgi, dysfunctional couple Little Tony and Ms. Peach, and Bromantic Puppies Boone and Kit.

I don't know which dog is to blame for our fleas and have questioned them repeatedly, but none of them is confessing.

Boone and Kit have asked for a lawyer.

Peach and Tony blame the cats.

Ruby claims it's a conspiracy, but that's

Fleas: 1; Puppies: 0

how corgis think. Paranoia is an occupational hazard for herding dogs, and let's be real, you never know when there's a wolf hiding around the corner to kill your sheep.

People, corgis are here to tell you. Keep an eye on your sheep.

I started noticing that the dogs were scratching a few months ago, or maybe it was last year. The thing about having a flea problem is that when you have it, you don't even remember your life before fleas. It's like life before Internet, happy and quiet.

We were happy, right?

I never had a flea problem before, so when

it first happened, I denied it. I simply pretended that it wasn't happening. This isn't hard to do if you just look the other way.

Until you start itching.

And then you want to burn your house down.

Seriously, when I found a flea on my leg, I couldn't wash my dogs fast enough. I had them in the tub every other day. I started out with the organic, all-natural flea shampoo, but when that didn't work, I segued into something radioactive.

Sometimes a girl needs a good pyrethrin.

And whoever banned DDT should be shot.

Just kidding.

Because the thing about a flea problem is that it doesn't mean washing only the dogs. It means washing your clothes, sheets, pillowcases, blankets, comforters, and any blankets on the chairs. It means the washing machine is running continuously and the rugs are being vacuumed constantly.

You may be wondering why this is so, and it's because fleas have a life cycle.

By the way, if you happen to be eating while you're reading this, you should either stop eating or stop reading, because what follows will disgust you.

The bottom line is that if you have a flea problem, you are going to wish you listened in Biology. You need to know about fleas, eggs, pupas, and larvae.

Disgusting.

Larvae is not a word you want in your life.

Much less in your bed.

By the way, larvae is the plural. I don't know what the singular is, and believe me, it doesn't matter. My experience with larvae is that there is never just one.

That's how larvae think.

They travel together, like wolves. Only you're the sheep.

See? Ruby is right again.

The most fun part of a flea problem is that you actually turn into a corgi, ever watchful, always on guard. I inspect myself constantly to make sure none of my moles are jumping.

I'm always combing through the dogs' fur with my fingers, in every nook and cranny. They told me they feel molested.

I scrutinize my sheets for telltale black dots, which are called flea dirt. Actually, the vet called it flea dirt, so I assumed that it was dirt that fell off fleas. But when I came home and looked it up online, I found out that it was actually flea poop.

First, who knew that fleas poop?

Second, disgusting.

See what I mean?

There is no bottom to any of this. Just when you thought it was as disgusting as it can get, it gets more disgusting.

Just ask the government.

FOR YOUR INFORMATION

BY LISA

Information is like turkey and stuffing.

It's hard to tell when you've had enough.

And the more you get, the more you want.

At least that's how I feel. I'm bad at portion control, whether it's Thanksgiving dinner or information.

Obviously, I don't believe there's such a thing as too much information. If you read this series, you know about my bunions, fleas, cellulite, and Mother Mary.

One of these is to be avoided at all costs.

Not the one you think.

FYI, I love information. I always want more. When I look back at my life, I know the things I wouldn't have done if I'd had more information. I'm talking Thing One, Thing Two, and Amway products.

But it turns out you can get more information than ever before, and I am giving thanks.

Because I heard about this kit you can

buy, test yourself, and find out your DNA.

I went to the website to learn about it, astounded. You order the kit, test your saliva, and send it back to the company.

Yes, you mail them your spit.

I'm wondering if I can mail them my cellulite, too.

Plus a few fleas.

Anyway, I am excited about this, and I ordered one for Daughter Francesca and one for me.

Merry Christmas, Francesca!

I don't know if Francesca wants a DNA kit for Christmas. If she doesn't, I'll take the test twice. Maybe my score will improve, like the SATs.

I didn't get a DNA kit for Mother Mary. I can find out what's in her DNA by looking in the mirror.

Also, can you imagine asking Mother Mary for a saliva sample?

"Here!" she'd say, and spit in my face.

So why do I want to do this? The test can let you know tons of things about yourself. For example, if you're a carrier of fifty-three different diseases, including Maple Syrup Urine Disease.

I bet you didn't even know that existed.

Neither did I.

Maybe Mrs. Butterworth had it.

I'm not sure what Maple Syrup Urine Disease is, but I'm guessing it's a disease that makes your urine look like maple syrup.

In that case, my medical advice would be simple.

Don't pee on your pancakes.

It may look right, but it won't taste right.

The test also lets you know if you're at risk for 122 diseases, including back pain.

Okay, maybe I already know that one.

The test can determine sixty of my genetic traits, but I already know a lot of those, too. For example:

Eye Color: Bloodshot Blue.

Hair Color: Fake.

Height: Stumpy.

Breast Morphology: Presently Morphing Due to Gravity and Unfairness of Life in General.

Memory: Huh?

Earwax Type: Johnson's.

Eating Behavior: Rapid and Unattractive.

Food Preference: Yes.

Caffeine Consumption: Dunkin' Donuts.

Odor Detection: How dare you.

Pain Response: Ouchy.

Muscle Performance: Slack and Wasting.

Response to Exercise: Procrastination.

Response to Diet: Not Applicable.

The test can even tell you whether you're

a carrier or at risk of a disease based on whether you originate from Europe, East Asia, or Africa. Sadly, there is no separate category for those of us who originate from South Philly.

Yo!

Interestingly, the kit can also tell you about your own ancestry. Both my mother and father were Italian-American, so I always assumed I was a purebred.

But maybe not.

And if I'm not Italian, somebody has to explain my nose.

The test can even determine what percent of my DNA comes from Neanderthals, which the website calls a Neanderthal Percentage.

I thought we all came from Neanderthals, but maybe not. Maybe there are other kinds of Thals.

The website says that Neanderthals have a bigger skull, which sounds exactly like me. Mother Mary always said I have a hard head, and now I have an excuse.

It's in my DNA.

In fact, it's her fault.

But will you be the one to tell her?

BACK TO SCHOOL
BY FRANCESCA

I wasn't sure what to expect for my five-year college reunion. All I knew was that it wasn't going to be a victory lap.

I feel lucky to have gone to Harvard. I got a great education, and I made a handful of very close friends and lasting connections with professors. But I didn't always love Harvard, and Harvard didn't always love me.

I had crazy roommates. I had a couple friendships that went down in flames.

I had one professor who hated my guts. I had many more who couldn't pick me out of a lineup.

I wasn't the president of any clubs. I co-founded one, but I left after my co-founder demoted me for rejecting his sexually offensive behavior.

I tried to have fun and find myself along the way, but mostly I worked my butt off and kept my head down.

So my thoughts about going to the reunion were mixed. But nervous energy and curiosity are closely related, and I had far too much of both to skip it.

The only thing I *wasn't* worried about was running into my college sweetheart. And not because I've matured beyond ex-boyfriend-anxiety — God no, do we ever grow out of that? — but because I knew he wouldn't be there. He's in the military and married. I expected the former would keep him too busy to come, and on the off chance he did show, the latter lent a finality that made things no longer interesting.

And anyway, I was much more intimidated to see ex-friends than ex-lovers. Women are ten times scarier than men. And I had some straight-up mean girls in my collegiate past. These were the interactions I was rehearsing in my head on the train ride up to Boston.

My plan was to take the high road, and take it fast. I wanted to rip off the Band-Aid and avoid an evening of side-eye over drinks. So I made a point to say hello to the Queen Bee as soon as I saw her.

She's a doctor now, so at least if she cut me, she could also stitch me up.

We shared a stiff hug and some small chat. It wasn't as bad as I thought.

I had the Hippocratic Oath on my side.

Or maybe she just didn't scare me anymore.

I counted that a win.

Later, a guy I sort-of knew, a biochemistry major, now PhD student, came over to say hello. I remembered him as nerdy but sweet. He was one of those guys you're not interested in when you're young, but then you think back on with a little regret. As we were chatting, I thought, maybe I had judged him too superficially, I bet he's going to make some girl really happy.

"So, are you married?" he asked.

"No. But I'm dating someone," I said.

"Are you engaged?"

I held up my bare hand. "Nope. Are you?"

"No, but," he placed his hand on my lower abdomen and said, "Clock is ticking."

I looked down at his hand and then up at him with a look that drained the color from his face.

"Sorry, that was weird," he said.

"Ye-ah." I backed away.

Some people are best left in the lab.

The rest of the evening, I had a good time with my friends, although most of them were the same people I still hang out regularly with in my adult life.

At the end of the night, in the ladies'-

With some friends who made Harvard wonderful

room line, I ran into a girl I knew only tangentially because she dated a friend of mine. In college, she seemed to have it all — she held a prestigious position in her activities, she did well in her classes, she was ambitious and outgoing. Back then I'd heard rumors she didn't like me, but because I have the type of self-esteem only an Italian mother can instill, I didn't believe it. How could she not like me when we hardly knew each other?

That she struck up a conversation with me now only seemed to confirm my sense that we were on the cusp of being friends. I greeted her warmly.

"So I just got to have a half-hour conversation with my asshole-ex-boyfriend. Isn't reunion the best?" she said.

Game for girl-bonding, I commiserated. "Exes are the worst. I'm lucky, my college boyfriend isn't here."

"I know who that is. You dated . . ." and she said my ex's full name for the whole line to hear, which struck me as edgy. Maybe we weren't about to become new pals.

She didn't leave me wondering long, as she added, "He's an assassin now, right?"

I recoiled. "He's serving in our armed forces, if that's what you mean."

"He shoots people out of an airplane, doesn't he? What's the difference?"

"There's a pretty big difference." With the "ABORT" alarm blinking in my brain, I tried to escape her when it was my turn in the restroom, but she found me again by the sinks. I refused to meet her eyes in the mirror, but I could feel her reflection glaring at me.

"He's married now, you know," she said.

I walked away; she followed. "I *do* know," I said, "and we're on good terms. I'm proud of him, and I wish him the best." I was now striding away from her, but she was literally jogging to keep up.

"They have a child, did you know *that*?"

I didn't. And hearing it from her first embarrassed me. But I was more flustered by this near stranger's animosity toward me and overinvolvement in my life. I turned to face her, held up my hand, and said only, "Stop."

She laughed in a weird way, and I wasted no time getting away from her. When there was some distance between us, I heard her shout:

"Their baby's name is Henry!"

I could only shake my head.

Thing is, I've moved on. My ex has moved on. For some reason, this girl had not.

I felt sorry for her.

So my reunion reminded me that college wasn't the best time of my life. The men there weren't my best options. My friendships weren't the best I would ever have. I wasn't my best self.

Thank goodness.

We Have a Winner

BY LISA

I just got back from a book tour through ten cities — including Las Vegas.

Jackpot!

Remarkably, I had never been to Vegas before.

I was a Vegas Virgin.

How did I get to go to Las Vegas on book tour?

I'm lucky.

Did I test this on my trip?

No. I didn't even step foot in a casino.

But I did get crazy in a Barnes & Noble.

Fun for bookworms!

So what happened?

Why didn't I lose my Vegas virginity?

Let me give you some background. The reason I got to go to Vegas was because I asked. I get a lot of email from fans who live there, and in twenty years of touring, I had never been to their town. They were beginning to feel dissed. One wrote me,

"People don't think we read in Las Vegas."

So I went, signed at the bookstore, and am here to tell you that people read in Las Vegas. Better yet, they read me, and that's all that really matters.

So did I gamble?

Well, I intended to. In fact, I was psyched. I had seen *The Hangover* three times, not only because Bradley Cooper is so crazy hot.

Oops. Did I say that out loud?

Anyway, if you've never been to Vegas, the fun begins on the plane. Everybody going to Vegas is in a great mood. I flew there from Minneapolis at ten in the morning, and everybody ordered a drink as soon as we had liftoff.

Or they did.

Only the hard core didn't party on the plane. They studied magazines about card-playing.

See, Vegas reads!

Anyway, I was ready to gamble. Anybody who knows my marital history knows this already.

And I could have started as soon as I got off the plane, because there were slot machines in the terminal. And near the ladies' room. And at baggage claim.

So efficient! You can lose your luggage and your retirement fund at the same time.

I figured I could gamble at my hotel, but when I checked in, I found out it didn't have a casino.

Evidently my publisher knows my marital history, too.

So I ate dinner and did the signing at the bookstore. It ended at nine o'clock, which left plenty of time to gamble. So why didn't I?

In my own defense, I tried.

I walked to the Bellagio, because a neon sign said that they had an exhibit of Andy Warhol paintings, and I figured that art would be a palate cleanser after all that commerce.

But when I saw how big the Bellagio was, I got intimidated. It was like Wegman's, only without the fun.

People were flooding in the big doors, which was when I also realized I don't know how to play poker. I don't know how you get the coins for the slot machines. I can't push my way to a roulette table; I can barely push my way to the deli counter.

I realized my gambling days were over.

Before they had even begun.

I work hard for my money, and I'd rather invest my earnings.

In shoes.

So I went back to the hotel, feeling vaguely

like a loser.

But when I got to my room, I had the time of my life.

In fact, I had the most fun you could have in Vegas, or anywhere else.

How?

I read a book.

Judge Not, Lest Ye Be a Pain in the Ass

BY LISA

Mother Mary always says, everybody's got problems.

Once again, she's right.

I say this because the other day, I was talking with a group of women and the conversation turned, as it naturally would, to our problems. One woman complained about her cholesterol problem, another about a mechanic who ripped her off, and I started complaining about how the cable repairman left without giving me a new remote.

Then somebody in the group said, "These are really First World problems."

And we all shut up, having been told that our problems didn't matter.

I myself didn't even know what that meant, but I wasn't about to say so in front of everybody else, having already been informed that my conversation was unworthy.

So I went home to look it up and found that First World problems are those experienced by people in wealthy, civilized countries, as compared with the problems experienced by people in Third World countries, like malaria.

Still I was kind of bugged, because everybody knows that the Third World has king-size problems, but that's not where we live.

So we have First World problems.

We never said we had Worst World problems.

They're still problems, to us.

And if we can't talk about First World problems, I might never utter another word.

Also, I wouldn't have anything to write about.

I read online that people were talking about rich-people problems and poor-people problems, and black-people problems and white-people problems and so on, but if you ask me, we're always being told to stop whining, even though we have an absolute, God-given right to whine.

And while we're on the subject, how annoying is it when the remote control doesn't work?

Yes, we're going to talk about that now, because it's still on my mind, and my bet is that it's on yours, too.

Granted it's not cholera, but don't you hate it when you have to push the OFF button four hundred times to turn the TV off?

And then through some mysterious mechanics in your remote, it turns off the cable but not the TV, or the TV but not the cable, and blue, green, and red lights are blinking like crazy? So you stretch your hand way up in the air and wave it back and forth like you're making semaphore signals, trying vainly to get the right angle on the TV and the cable box so that you can finally turn them both off at the same time and get to sleep?

I know it won't kill me, but honestly.

Do you really expect those of us in the First World to walk to the TV and turn it off?

We can't even find the button.

We hire people to do that for us.

Also, why don't they make a remote control that lights up at night, so you can see the ON and OFF buttons in the dark?

Daughter Francesca has one of those in New York, and it's awesome. Yet those of us in the First-and-a-Half World, namely the Philadelphia suburbs, have to hit three hundred different buttons at the top of the remote, praying that one of them is the OFF

43

button, but instead is the AUX button, whatever that is, or the SETUP button, so we can screw up our television permanently by setting the language to Czechoslovakian.

You guessed it, this is what I was whining about when someone reminded me that people are starving in Africa.

Yet you're probably having the exact same problem with your remote control, or a series of related problems, as remotes manifest an array of maladies, none of which involves tsetse flies.

Also, it drives the dogs nuts when the remote control doesn't work because they sleep clustered around me, and every time I start sitting up and waving the remote control, they get disrupted and it ruins their beauty sleep.

Yes, I have First World dogs.

American dogs.

You got a problem with that?

I don't.

CITY MOUSE, COUNTRY CAT

BY FRANCESCA

It was like the opening scene of a horror film. I was playing the oblivious blonde chatting with her friend over the phone, home alone — or so I thought. The minute I end the call, I see it: a flash of movement in the dark corner of my living room. Fear flickers across my face, but I shake it off, while any sentient audience member wants to yell at the screen.

But I start to look, first casually, then frantically, for the intruder that, deep down, I know I saw. Using the flashlight of my iPhone camera, I shine a light behind every door, around every corner. I flatten myself on the ground and squeeze myself under the couch, fumbling to bring the flashlight app back up for one excruciating minute, and when it finally turns on . . .

The mouse is right in front of my face.

Don't believe me? I took a picture. The mouse was so audacious in staring me down that it stood for a portrait session.

That's a city mouse for you.

I've dealt with his kind before. Mice are a horror movie, and there's always a sequel. The original *Squeak* was set in my old apartment in a crummier building that sat above two restaurants. The mice there were so well established, they paid rent.

But my new apartment is better run, so I thought I'd be protected from *Squeak 2, I Know What You Ate Last Summer.*

The mouse appeared the day I was leaving for Thanksgiving, so I hastily set a few wooden traps, snapping them on my finger only twice, and rushed to make my train.

At home, I was telling my mom the story at the kitchen island, when one of our cats, Mimi, sprang onto the countertop.

A lightbulb went off.

I'd take this country cat back to the city with me as an all-natural, rodent-killing machine.

It seemed like a perfect plan. I love Mimi, and Mimi loves mice. What she doesn't love is living with the mini-mafia of five dogs in my mom's house. I have only one dog, Pip, and he hardly counts.

My only concern was the kitty-litter smell in a small apartment. So I went to Petco to educate myself on deodorizing.

Kitty litter is way more confusing than it needs to be. Only the Sphinx could answer the riddle of kitty litter, and even she gave up and opted for plain sand.

How am I supposed to choose between Tidy Cat Instant Action and Tidy Cat 24/7 Performance? I don't want to smell cat excrement now *or* later. Why not combine the technology? Is this a conspiracy to make me buy both? Arm & Hammer Double Duty litter touts that it eliminates feces *and* urine odors. Isn't that a given? Rare is the customer who thinks, "Cat pee is the worst, but cat poop — not bad."

Overwhelmed by choice, I went overboard. I bought a covered litter box with an air filter at the top, scented liners, deodorizing powder, and whichever litter brand was nearest when I got tired of trying to make sense of them. Not to mention all the fun stuff I bought for my new pet, like toys, food bowls, and a little flowered collar with a personalized tag.

At checkout, I wondered if this was actually cheaper than hiring an exterminator.

Still, I was excited. Mimi was going to solve my mouse problem and be a beloved addition to my little family.

But Mimi did not rest at all during the three-hour drive back to the city. She crouched at the back of the crate with eyes the size of saucers. I started to worry the country-to-city transition wouldn't be as easy on her as I'd thought.

I made it back to my apartment dragging my suitcase, the dog on a leash, the cat carrier under my arm, and what felt like sixty pounds of deodorizing, multicat, extra-strength, instant and round-the-clock kitty litter.

As soon as I opened the front door, a putrid stench struck me like an olfactory freight train.

Dead mouse.

One of my wooden traps had worked, and a while ago, by the smell of things.

I opened the cat carrier and Mimi instantly fled deep into my closet. Pip chased after her. The mouse was dead as a doornail.

The kitty litter, however, smelled fine.

Baby Me
BY LISA

My life just got awesome.
  Yours can, too.
  What changed my life?
  The perfect chair.
  In the movie theater.
  I'm not even kidding.
  Relax.
  Sit down.
  In the perfect chair.
  At the *movies.*
They say you should enjoy the simple things in life, and I do, and so did everybody else last night, when my Best Friend Franca and I went to the movies and as soon as we walked into the theater, we saw that it had been completely transformed.

The filthy rug on the floor had been replaced with a clean maroon-patterned rug, and the walls had been repainted a matching color, but best of all, instead of the narrow straight-backed chairs that used

49

to be in the rows were half as many chairs — and they were all as wide as a love seat.

It was as if the entire theater had gone from coach to first class.

Free.

Wow.

We couldn't believe our eyes. We stopped in our tracks.

The seats were double-wide and they would fit double-wide butts perfectly.

And the chairs were not only huge, but they were covered with some type of gray upholstery, either leather-like cloth or cloth-like leather, but let's not be picky.

Does life get better than this?

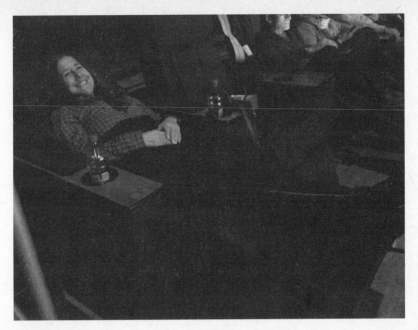

Bestie Franca and I know how to relax.

Franca and I started giggling, and everybody else felt exactly the same way, because we all just stood there marveling at the massive gray chairs, oohing and ahhing like tourists at Stonehenge, if the monoliths were soft.

Then all at once, we all bolted for the big chairs, jumping into them and finding to our delight that not only were they double-wide, but if you hit a button on the armrest, the back reclined all the way, so it lay completely flat.

O.M.G.

And the seat cushion was thick as a mattress, cushy, and vaguely Craftmatic.

Plus, if you hit a button on the other side of the armrest, the lower half of the seat rose to elevate your feet completely.

In other words, it was a *bed.*

At the movies.

Franca and I looked at each other in astonishment, then we started hitting buttons like crazy, making the seatback go down and the footrest go up and generally playing with the buttons like the three-year-old boys we never were.

And everybody around us was doing the same thing, forty-, fifty-, and sixty-year-olds playing with the buttons, making their feet and heads go up and down, laughing, taking pictures of themselves and each other in the seats, emailing and texting the pictures to their friends, and calling their children to report that a miracle had taken place and recliners had landed at the movie theater.

Okay, maybe only Franca and I took pictures and emailed them to our children.

We tried to call them, too, but they weren't in.

Because it was Saturday night and they had better things to do than take calls from their crazy mothers who were playing with their new toys.

But wait, there's more, because this bed

at the movies had what every bed should have, everywhere in the world.

Bradley Cooper.

Just kidding.

What these beds had were cupholders.

And not a teeny tiny cupholder, but a big circle that was wide enough to fit a Diet Coke and a box of Raisinets in the same hole. And the armrest itself was so wide that we both could put a bag of popcorn on it, like a shelf.

What?

Does life get better than this?

No.

And just then, the manager of the theater materialized and asked us if we were enjoying our "theater experience," to which I answered:

"You're darn tootin'!"

Then he said, "If you wish, you can push away that armrest between and that will transform the seat into a sofa. We call it the cuddle seat."

"Good to know," I told him, declining because Franca and I have been friends for thirty years and we cuddle quite enough, thank you.

In time, the overhead lights went off and the previews came on, and everybody put their phones away and settled down, pushing the buttons to make their footrest go back down and reclining their backrest only a reasonable degree.

Everybody, that is, but Franca and me.

We stayed in our twin beds, watching the movie.

It was totally fun and great.

The chairs, not the movie.

In fact, the chairs were better than the movie, but I didn't care because I was having the time of my life,

I managed to drink my soda lying flat on my back and didn't spill any more popcorn than usual on my chest.

By the end of the movie, I was wearing Raisinets.

So that's a tiny problem.

Maybe next time the manager will feed me.

THE REAL ME
BY FRANCESCA

A new year can be about reinventing yourself. This year, many women decided to become a whole new person:

Me.

I was the victim of "high-level identity theft."

It began when I came home from the holidays to find twelve new credit cards opened in my name, none by me. Somebody had gotten my social security number, birth date, and address.

I freaked. I called my mom, and she freaked. Then I calmed down and looked online. I learned I could resolve the fraud in, oh, about one hundred easy steps.

The first was to file a police report. Simply being inside the police precinct made me feel guilty. I felt guilty for being a boring case. I felt guilty for making paperwork. I felt guilty that I had no leads.

If I'd waited any longer, I'd have made a

false confession.

I was told to go see the detective on the second floor. Outside of his office was a wall of WANTED posters with illustrations and surveillance shots for criminals of every sort, all in my neighborhood. It was like an inspiration board for nightmares.

Or Police Pinterest.

I gulped and went inside.

The detective didn't share my shock about identity theft. He waved a hand, and said, "They've got such sophisticated methods now, everyone's social has been compromised. It's just bad luck that your number came up."

Go figure. I finally have the right numbers, and somebody else gets rich.

Next, I set about calling the credit bureaus and customer-service lines for all the fraudulent accounts. It took six hours, but I got a better understanding of what happened.

Sometime mid-December, multiple women in several states used my identity to do a little holiday shopping — or a lot — nearly $10,000. They'd open a credit card at a retail store and max it out the same day. On a few occasions, the imposters were denied. Some of the mistakes that foiled these criminal masterminds were: misspelling my name, getting my gender wrong, or listing "Serritella" as my first name and "Francesca" as my last.

Confusing ethnic name for the win!

A fraud representative informed me that one thief, after being initially denied, had called the customer-service line to try to "verify" her identity.

I mean, *my identity.*

"That one had some *cojones,*" the representative said.

For some reason it really bothers me that it was women who impersonated me. It's sexist, but when I think of a criminal, I envision a man, or if I do think of a female criminal, I imagine a woman destroying a man's property, justifiably so — Carrie Underwood and her Louisville-Slugger-type stuff. Identity theft must be a major violation of the Girl Code.

Hook up with my ex-boyfriend, but leave my credit score alone. And yet, woman-on-woman crime is so predictable. It triggers the catty, mean-girl thoughts I otherwise keep suppressed. Like when I imagine some chick sticking her picture on a phony ID with *my* pristine credit info to buy her stupid girl-stuff from Old Navy, Home Goods, Victoria's Secret, Nordstrom . . .

She's probably not even cute!

Last year, my credit-card information was stolen and used at a grocery store. That inspired sympathy in me. It was like Jean Valjean ripped off my credit card to buy a loaf of bread.

These latest thefts are nonessential. I mean, Home Goods?

I'm so glad my identity was stolen so that you could buy a *decorative pillow.*

Karma says, if you commit fraud to buy a scented candle, you'll burn your house down with it.

Recently, the detective emailed me a surveillance photo of one of the women using my identity. I didn't recognize her. I felt bad I couldn't help the investigation, but I'm relieved that I don't have con-women for friends.

The woman was very voluptuous. With the camera angle, I was nearly looking down her shirt. Believe me, no one could mistake her for me.

I wish.

No wonder she spent over a grand at Victoria's Secret.

Even in the grainy photo, I could tell that she was wearing false lashes. I didn't like that. In my opinion, false lashes are trying too hard. They never look real.

Not that this would concern an identity thief.

But please, if you're going to impersonate me, try to look your best.

Or mine.

TASK MASTER

BY LISA

The other day, somebody asked me if I was "task-oriented."

I replied, "Proudly."

I have no problem being task-oriented.

In fact, I love being task-oriented.

You know why?

It gets things done.

So what if I have a gaping ulcer?

Every bowel needs a little ventilation.

In my opinion, life is full of tasks, and only the task-oriented have the proper orientation to get all the tasks done.

You can take a test to see if you're task-oriented, in the privacy of your own home. In fact, I developed the test myself, and it consists of answering two questions, which are contained in Part I and Part II.

That's not a very hard test, is it?

You don't even have to study.

Here's Part I, and the question assumes that you had a Christmas tree, because that's how I came to the realization that helped me develop this test. If you did not have a Christmas tree, or in other words if you are Jewish, Muslim, Buddhist, or an extremely lazy Christian, please accept my apologies and imagine that you did have a Christmas tree, so you can take the test anyway.

If you're an agnostic, you need to make up your mind. Stop dithering. Pick a team. Don't wait until the end. You might get caught out. It may not be good to wear a Giants jersey at the Eagles game, but it's better than going naked.

Baby, it's cold outside.

If you're an atheist, you're on your own. After all, that's what you wanted, isn't it? Be careful what you wish.

Okay, now to Part I, Question 1.

The question is, When do you take down your Christmas tree?

The answer is multiple-choice, so please pick one of the following:

A) A few days after Christmas.
B) The day after New Year's.
C) When the kids go back to school.
D) When it dies, when I'm sick of my feet getting stuck by pine needles, or when birds begin to nest in it, whichever

61

comes first.

E) None of the above, and if so, please explain. Show your work.

Okay, got your answer?
Write it down, but don't tell it to me.
Cover your paper with your hand, so nobody cheats off you.
I'll tell you my answer when the test is over.
I don't want you to cheat off me. The task-oriented are always right. Just ask them.
Er, I mean, us.
Okay, let's move on to Part II, Question 1.

The question is, Regardless of when you *actually* took down your Christmas tree, when did you *want* to take down your Christmas tree?

A) After Christmas dinner, when
   everybody is comatose on the couch.
B) After Christmas breakfast, when
   everybody is watching the football game.
C) As soon as the kids turn their backs.
D) As soon as the presents are unwrapped.
E) Before the presents are unwrapped.
F) Christmas Eve.
G) None of the above, because I'm sane.

Okay, do you have your answer?

Pencils down.

Here are the results.

Part I, Question 1 of the test doesn't matter. It was a trick question, but in a good way. Whatever answer you gave is correct, because if you're a nice person, married, or otherwise live in a family, you might not have been able to bend them to your task-oriented will.

We're bossy, not tyrannical.

Part II, Question 1 of the test is the only part that matters, and if your answer was A through F, you're certifiably task-oriented!

Welcome to the club!

Thank God your family has you to rush them through the happiest time of the year, so they can get it over with and move on to doing their taxes.

Here's what I'm saying to you.

I realized I was task-oriented when I *could not wait* to take down the Christmas tree, put all the ornaments away, vacuum up all the stupid needles, and put a check mark in the box next to Christmas on my Things To Do List, so I could get back to work.

Feel the same way?

Got Maalox?

OLD AND NEW
BY LISA

It's the New Year, and they say, "Out with the Old, and in with the New."

But I disagree.

I don't think we have to get rid of the Old to bring in the New.

You'll disagree, too.

If you're Old.

I think Old and New can live together, in peace, at the same time. For example, the Christmas tree that Daughter Francesca and I decorated this year had a bunch of New ornaments but plenty of Old, if not Ancient, ones like:

A wooden reindeer with one remaining eye and only two legs, which I bought for Francesca when she was two;

A red glass ball with the word "Joy" written in glitter, which Francesca made in middle school for a beloved horse who passed away;

A twenty-year-old glass snowman whose

eye was so worn away that we drew in a new one with a Sharpie; and

A little wooden tree that has three clay golden retrievers with the names of our goldens Lucy, Angie, and Penny, all of whom have passed away.

You get the idea.

If you're maimed or dead, you're on our tree.

See what I mean?

Old is good.

Old is sweet.

Old still matters.

Same with our Christmas music. When we open gifts on Christmas morning, we always play the Charlie Brown CD on a continuous loop, even though it's twenty-five years old and skips like a record.

Please tell me you know what a record is.

Still, we never get sick of hearing it. Francesca knows every note, and I know every skip.

And for the meal, we wanted to make something New, which we hadn't made before, so we found a recipe to honor my late father, whose parents lived in Ascoli Piceno, Italy. The region is known for its stuffed olives, and Francesca found an Old recipe, one that's been around for hundreds of years.

Unfortunately, it took hundreds of years to make it.

First we made the stuffing, then stuffed a zillion olives, then breaded the olives, then fried the olives, etc., etc., etc. We even had help from my bestie Franca, who came over for dinner, whom you may recall I have known for thirty years.

We have the right idea when it comes to friends, with that saying, "Make new friends but keep the old."

So let's choose one cliché over the other, shall we? And banish that "out with the Old."

I say this because I often feel that older people aren't appreciated enough for their experience, wisdom, and perspective. There's entirely too much sweeping away of the Old in this culture.

I know many of you agree, even if you're not Old.

And as we get older, many of us experience the feeling of being marginalized or sidelined, simply because of our age.

I've seen Mother Mary condescended to and patronized in public, which drives me crazy.

Dis me, but don't be dissing my mother.

Because time and space, as they relate to people, are completely beside the point.

The Old are always with us, as are those who are no longer alive, whether they're dogs or fathers.

We don't stop loving them, nor do we stop remembering them. Boundaries dissolve, and definitions merge, because those things are meaningless, too.

Nothing Old need be swept aside, to make room for the New.

There's plenty of room in the human heart for all of us.

Happy New Year.

BETTOR FOR WORSE

BY FRANCESCA

If you start betting on guilty-pleasure television, does that make it guiltier?

I created a fantasy league for *The Bachelor.*

The Bachelor, for those who pretend they've never seen it, is a dating game show in which thirty women vie for the love of one man, and after a mere eight weeks of choreographed dates, rose-ceremony eliminations, and much artful editing, he chooses one true love to make his wife.

It's about as progressive as it sounds, and yet, it's compelling enough to last eighteen seasons and counting.

Fantasy-*Bachelor* is just like fantasy football, but with more crying.

I figured upping the ante would make watching the show more fun, so I recruited a few other friends who also enjoy *The Bachelor* ironically (yeah right, we just like it) to join in my pool.

Turns out, being a bettor made me worse.

I thought I liked *Bachelor* because I'm a romantic. But when I had money on it, I became a cynic.

My strategy was that Juan-Pablo would base his choices on sexual attraction alone. He constantly talked about wanting a stepmother for his daughter, but I wasn't buying it. I put only one of the single mothers in my top five, and she was at the bottom.

I don't have money to waste on fairy tales.

Which was good, because Juan-Pablo was no Prince Charming.

I chose Clare as my number one pick, because Juan-Pablo was all over her from the start. If he weren't so handsome, the word would be *lecherous.*

Don't hate the player, hate the game. Or game show.

After weeks of Juan-Pablo sticking his tongue in Clare's mouth every time she talked, she initiated a clandestine midnight swim . . . *et cetera,* an offer he took her up on without hesitation. But the very next day, he chastised her for inappropriately sneaking extra time with him and going "too far."

Any other season, I would've been shouting at my TV screen for Clare to leave this hypocrite. This time, I had the empathy of Bobby Knight.

Get over it, Clare, we have a game to win.

She forgave him. And from then on, Juan-Pablo's bad behavior played into my bets perfectly.

When his dopey conversation irritated Sharleen enough to bail — great, I had her down as the one to leave of her own accord.

When his narcissism became a deal breaker for Andi — even better, I always had her in the third-place spot.

Juan-Pablo's wrongs were all right with me.

Finally, the unmagical journey was at its end. The two remaining were my star player, Clare, and Nikki, a dark horse I didn't have anywhere on my team. The stakes were high.

For me and my ten bucks, not for the people choosing a spouse on TV.

I invited my girlfriend and fellow fantasy-league competitor over to watch the finale, a typically bloated and boring episode.

Not this time.

Juan-Pablo outdid himself, whispering something to Clare in the helicopter — always a helicopter — that, according to her, was so disgusting and offensive, she couldn't repeat it.

My friend and I had a field day trying to guess what it was.

But then Clare cried. And I was reminded

this wasn't a fantasy league of well-compensated professional athletes. These were women like me.

Okay, like me but with better hair and makeup.

Ultimately, after endlessly jerking her around, Juan-Pablo rejected Clare. And she wouldn't hug him.

Instead, she told him off in the best way possible.

As she said on the after-show, "I had never been able to stand up for myself to a man before. It was so liberating to be able to stand there and say, this is exactly how I feel, and it's not okay."

We were so proud of her, we applauded the TV.

Twitter exploded, along with my fantasy bracket.

But I've never felt so genuinely happy at the end of a *Bachelor* season. For once, the show and the viewing audience seemed to be on the side of the real woman, instead of just the fantasy.

I lost.

Women won.

GEARED UP!
BY LISA

They say that you never forget how to ride a bicycle.

Once again, they don't know what they're talking about.

I say this because I got a bicycle for Christmas. And I forgot how to ride one.

In fairness to me, this bicycle came with a fifty-four-page instruction booklet and a CD.

Let me first say that I love my gift, which was given to me by my bestie Laura. I know how lucky I am to have a great friend like her, as well as a cool new bike. So don't think I'm ungrateful, but I never thought I'd have to study to ride a bike.

Isn't Step One, Put butt on seat?

Step Two, Point front end forward?

Step Three, Place feet on black things?

Step Four, Press down.

Step Five, Don't fall.

If only it were that easy.

857,938 gears, but no kickstand!

The last time I rode a bicycle was in high school, which was forty years ago. When I got the new bike, I hopped on and tried to ride it around the driveway. I managed not to fall, but I was no Lance Armstrong.

Except not even Lance Armstrong is Lance Armstrong anymore.

Bottom line, nothing about bicycles is the way I remember.

I realized this as soon as I tried to brake by pedaling backwards and almost rode into a tree.

What happened to coaster brakes?

Were they too perfect and too simple to

survive the modern era?

I know there's such a thing as hand brakes, but I couldn't find them on the short black stick that is now called the handlebar. My old handlebars curved around to meet me like a warm hug, but this new handlebar is something you have to lean forward to put your hands on. You know you're in the correct position when your back spasms.

And when you look up to see where you're going, you can break your own neck.

Wow!

These new bicycles are so technologically sophisticated, you don't even have to crash to injure yourself.

Plus, I can barely perch on the hard sliver of black plastic they want me to use for a seat. My old bike used to have a cushy black seat shaped like one of those paddles they use for pizza. In fact, my old seat was big enough to accommodate the butt I get from eating pizza.

I miss my old bike seat. If I could stick a Barcalounger on a bike, I would. Maybe I need a recumbent bike, or Craftmatic adjustable bed on wheels.

Then there's the matter of adjusting my new bicycle. The bike allegedly came adjusted, but sitting on the seat was like a do-it-yourself Pap smear.

I tried to figure out how to lower the seat, but I couldn't understand the manual, so I tried to lower the handlebar instead. But I couldn't figure that out from the manual either, and this is why. The manual said, "Your bike is equipped either with the threadless stem, which clamps onto the outside of the steerer tube, or with a quill stem, which clamps inside the steerer tube by way of an expanding binder bolt."

What?

The manual told me to ask my dealer whether I had a threadless stem or a quill stem, but I'm not asking my dealer.

He doesn't know me that well.

Also, "steerer" isn't an adjective, no matter how you slice it.

I thumbed through the rest of the manual to learn about the gears on my new bike. I remember that my old bike had three gears, which were: the one I always use, the one I hope to use, and the one I will never use.

Then I remember when ten-speed bikes were invented, a certifiable scientific advance. I begged my parents to get me one, and they did, but I never used any gears beyond the aforementioned first three.

My new bike has 857,938 gears.

Guess how many I will use.

MOTHER MARY
GETS RELIGION
BY LISA

I'm worried about Mother Mary.

Because she found religion.

In a manner of speaking, anyway.

We begin when Brother Frank tells me that he'll call me on Sunday, "after church."

I don't understand. No Scottoline has gone to church in centuries, least of all my mother, who was excommunicated from the Catholic Church after she got divorced and remarried.

Can you imagine Catholicism without a Mother Mary?

I asked, "Frank, did you and Mom start going to church?"

"No, I meant we watch on TV."

"You and Mom watch church on television?"

"Yes, every Sunday morning, we watch Mass together."

I don't understand this. I didn't know this was possible. Church on TV? Are there commercials? "Why did you start doing this?"

"Mom wants to. It was her idea."

"Why?"

"I don't know."

I ask a few more questions and ascertain that they started a few months ago, and though I feel touched, I'm also worried. My mother isn't in the best of health and though her mind is as quick as ever, lately her speech has slowed. She has a speech therapist, and her doctors say there's no cause for alarm, but still, I wonder if the TV-church thing means she is worrying.

I'm worrying about her worrying.

If she's worried, then I'll be doubly worried. Maybe triple. If you didn't think you could quadruple-worry, you haven't been a daughter.

Or a mother.

So I tell Frank to put Mother Mary on the phone, which he does. "Mom, do you and Frank really watch church on Sunday mornings?"

"Who wants to know?"

I let that go, because you may remember that Mother Mary always answers a question with a question. "Why are you doing this?"

"Do I have to have a reason?"

"No, but if you have a reason, I'd like to know it."

"Why do you want to know? You have to have a reason for asking me what my reason is."

Now I'm getting confused. "I'm just curious."

"I like it. That's the reason, okay? It makes me feel good. Is that a good enough reason for you?"

"Yes."

Mother Mary snorts. "I'm glad you approve."

I feel heartened. If she's sarcastic, she's fine. "Mom, I have an idea. If you want, Frank can take you to church. I looked it up online and there's a church three miles from your house."

"No, I don't want to go."

"Why not?"

"What's it to you?"

"Well, it seems like part of going to church is being part of the community, and you might like it more if you went, instead of watching it on television."

"I don't want to be part of a community."

"But it would be fun, Mom. You can get to know the people, meet the priest, and get out of the house."

"I don't want to meet anybody or get out

of the house."

I switch gears. "Okay, how about this? I did a little research and I found out that there are ministers from the church who will actually come to your house and visit you, if you want."

"I don't want a minister to visit me."

"Why not?"

"Why are you asking me all these questions?" Mother Mary blows her top. "Do you want ministers visiting you? Are you going to church? What community are you part of?"

I sigh inwardly. "Okay, fair point. It just seems like it's second-best to watch it on TV."

"Why? What do you watch Sunday mornings?"

"Meet the Press."

"Why do you watch that?"

"It's important."

Mother Mary snorts again. "You want to know what's important? Watch church."

HOWDY NEIGHBOR
BY FRANCESCA

I'm currently sitting in front of my computer not wearing a bra. This is pretty standard for me, not usually an issue, except I just made eye contact with a construction worker standing one foot outside my window.

I've got scaffolding problems.

Construction is a fact of life in New York City. Real estate is to New York as oil is to Texas, it's where all the money is, and for real-estate barons, maintaining and improving their most valuable asset takes precedence over any resident's needs.

Capital capital trumps human capital every time.

Excuse me, Trumps™.

I was used to construction noise, the jackhammering, the beeping as trucks reverse, the once-concerning booms and bangs. I walk through a neighborhood in perpetual semidemolition without a second thought.

It's debatable whether or not I need a hard hat to walk the dog.

The sounds still alarm my mother, even when she hears them over the telephone.

"Are you okay?" she'll cry. "What was that?"

"Hm? Oh, they're destroying a preschool to build another Marc Jacobs."

Alarming, but in a different way.

I didn't fully appreciate how awful construction could be until it hit close to home.

About four inches from my home, to be exact.

Without warning, the management started some surface renovations to the façade of my building this spring. I live in a small duplex on the ground floor, my bedroom sits on the lower level, and the first thing the crew did was rip out the wrought-iron fence outside my bedroom windows.

At first, I was delighted. Food delivery-men serving my neighbors' late-night cravings often chained their bikes on that fence, and the sound of jangling chains would wake me up.

It was like the ghost of Jacob Marley was coming to bring me vegetable lo mein — dual harbingers of regret.

So, I was pro construction! Until the next

Oh hey, guys.

morning, when I awoke to steel scaffolding being hammered into the exterior wall.

The noise made a bike-chain sound like wind chimes.

The following morning, I thought my clock was wrong — quarter to eight and completely dark outside? Then I realized my apartment had been mummified.

They had wrapped the outside of my apartment with a thick mesh netting to protect it from whatever Smash Bros. "improvements" they were doing to the exterior.

I was living inside a gypsy-moth nest.

Upstairs, things really got awkward. The scaffolding is level with my second floor, so the workmen look like they're *in* my living room.

Sitting at my desk beside my window, they're so close I feel like I should offer them a soda.

What's the social etiquette here? If I don't acknowledge them, I feel like a snob. If I do acknowledge them, it's like I'm on an all-day blind date.

With six men. For the next eight weeks.

Even closing my windows feels personal, like I'm closing it in their face. For the first two weeks, I said, "sorry" every time.

How about the etiquette on their end? Getting checked out by construction workers is a hazard for any woman, but I'm not used to it when I'm sitting on my couch.

To be fair, the crew has been respectful. They don't smile or interact with me when I'm inside the apartment.

However, as soon as I walk outside, all bets are off.

When I heard one mutter something behind me on the sidewalk, I wanted to turn around and say, "We'll talk about this when we get home."

So I feel a low level of self-consciousness all day. When I'm eating at my table, I use my restaurant manners instead of my lives-alone manners.

Don't act like you don't know what I'm talking about.

Dreams do come true.

And when I'm writing at my desk, I try to look busy and not surf the Internet.

So maybe it's not such a bad thing.

The main inconvenience is I've had to dress better — or, more — during my workday.

People who go to an office every day may not understand, but I work at home; dressing like a homeless person who may have a gym membership is not just my choice, it's my right.

Believe me, if I wanted to wear pants to work, I'd have a job that offered health insurance.

I should have a needlepoint pillow that says, "Home is where the bra comes off."

So, I decided, screw it. Deal with it, boys. I'm working here.

And as if by magic, my super told me the scaffolding comes down tomorrow.

Because nobody wants to see that.

Home improved.

FIGHT THE POWER

BY LISA

Now is not the winter of our discontent.

Now is the winter of our stressed-to-the-max, pull-out-our-hair, if-we-get-more-snow-I'll-move-to-Florida. Because we have lost heat, electric, and Internet, and we have salted, shoveled, and plowed through snow, sleet, and ice.

But to me, the problem isn't heat.

It's ventilation.

As in, we need to vent about how much this winter sucks.

Who says talking about the weather is boring?

All I want to talk about is the weather.

I'm lucky enough to have a generator, but it didn't work in the beginning even though it cost a small fortune. Then when I finally got it working, I had light and heat only in the kitchen, where I had a laptop and a refrigerator.

And a burglar alarm.

To protect the refrigerator.

Also I had a book deadline, because I arrange my book deadlines to occur at the worst possible times for my continued solvency.

I got enough propane refills to keep me working for six days, during which I had no Internet or cable, no communication with the outside world except when I called my electric company, which was very concerned about my power outage.

I know, because their recorded message told me so.

All monopolies have recorded messages that tell you how much they care about you.

It's like the worst marriage ever.

To a really controlling robot.

Who can only estimate how much he costs you, but it's still way too much.

Every night I called and followed their mechanical prompts to plug in my phone number, tell them I was still out of power, and find out when my power would be back. And every day, the recording told me that my power would be restored in two days. Then I realized that no matter when I called, they always said the power would be on in two days.

It wasn't a deadline.

It was a dead lie.

Two days turned out to be like the twenty minutes they tell you to trick you into staying on the phone for technical support, or into waiting for a table in a restaurant, or into filling out this simple and easy credit application.

We are all rendered powerless by our power company.

They win every power struggle.

Because they have the power.

Day after day, I stuck it out, living in my coat and forehead flashlight, like a demented gynecologist.

When the eighth day came, I made my deadline but I still had no Internet connection and couldn't email my book to my publisher.

So I packed my laptop and fled to Daughter Francesca's apartment in New York City, which always has power.

It's a powerful town.

You know why New York always has heat, light, and shoveled sidewalks?

Lawyers.

Every building owner knows he will get his ass sued if you fall on yours.

As a result, snow is salted, shoveled, and plowed before it hits the ground. Really, people are hired to run around and catch snowflakes in their cupped hands.

The lawyers keep New York hermetically sealed in a cushioned bubble, like Planet Manhattan, and the only problem with Planet Manhattan is that no one there wants to hear you vent.

They will listen for about one minute.

The proverbial New York Minute.

So I emailed my book to my publisher, met my deadline, and kissed my beloved daughter good-bye.

I came home to Pennsylvania.

Where I'm happy to listen to you vent.

Go for it.

Your feedback is very important to us.

THE TRUTH TASTES DELICIOUS
BY LISA

I'm trying to lose weight and I wonder if I need a nutritionist.

Or a miracle.

Our story begins when I notice I've gained seven pounds over the winter.

This can't be my fault.

I blame the snow.

Don't you?

Let's all blame the snow!

And instead of running around with yardsticks, we'll use tape measures. In fact, we should redo the snowfall maps on the TV weather report and put up the inches we gained on our waistlines.

Six inches in Chester County?

Wow!

And it's sticking?

To my butt!

I didn't even realize I'd gained weight until I had to get dressed for a speaking engagement, which meant I had to unpeel the fleece sweatsuit I'd worn through November, December, and January, and put on clothes that had actual seams.

Not possible.

In February, seams are not your friend.

Turns out, neither are zippers or buttons.

I guess I was fooled because my fleece sweatsuit is black.

So slimming.

In it, I look like a licorice jellybean.

Delicious.

Anyway, to stay on point, I was going to wear a wool blazer with my nice jeans, but neither fit at all. Even my boots didn't fit, because my calves had gotten bigger.

Here is what fit:

My gloves.

Luckily, my fingers retained their girlish figure.

It was a foregone conclusion that I couldn't get into my jeans, because I can't get into my jeans unless the stars align, but I knew I was in trouble when my boots wouldn't go on.

And then I couldn't button my blazer.

What's a jellybean to do?

I changed into a double-breasted jacket and buttoned it on the outer button, so it looked like a maternity wear for the menopausal.

But after my gig, I got serious and wanted to start a diet, but I didn't know which one. Also, at the same time, I wanted to stop eating anything unnatural, like fake sugar.

Plus I'm also vegetarian.

That means there's one thing I can eat.

But I don't know what it is.

I had gone on the South Beach Diet before, but that's kind of meaty, and I'd read a book called *Wheatbelly* about eating less wheat, but I didn't think that would help, since I had an *Everything-Belly.*

So I tried to cut down on my caloric intake and had a hard-boiled egg for breakfast, a bowl of soup for lunch, and a kale salad for dinner.

What happened?

I couldn't stick to the diet, and after a week, I was eating tons of pasta for dinner, and for dessert, dumping raw sugar in my coffee and practically bathing in salted caramels from Whole Foods.

Whoever invented putting salt on sweets was an evil genius.

I gained two pounds.

And I began craving salty/sweet things at night.

Like Bradley Cooper.

Just kidding.

Kind of.

I tried to educate myself on nutrition by ordering more books and watching an online video by a Dr. Robert Lustig, called *Sugar: The Bitter Truth.* And I learned that instead of blaming the snow, I should have been blaming the sugar.

The video had been viewed 4,359,323 people, which meant I was the 4,359,324th to learn the following:

Sugar is bad. Don't eat sugar. Fructose is bad. Don't eat fruct.

Ghrelin is the hunger hormone, and fructose does not suppress ghrelin. Nothing suppresses ghrelin except salted caramels.

Fructose is not glucose even though they rhyme.

Leptin is a hormone that tells your brain you're full. I suspect I am fresh out of leptin, and they don't sell it at Whole Foods.

And the bitter truth?

I need something else to blame.

The sweet truth?

I have a sweet tooth.

STILL HERE, KITTY?

BY FRANCESCA

For the first two days of my new life as a cat-owner, I did not see my cat. Just take my word for it, I had one, an absentee cat named Mimi, not that she answers to it. I knew she existed because the kitty litter was periodically disturbed, but it could've been my dog, Pip, working on a Zen garden.

I recently repo'd one of our family cats from my mom in order to catch a particularly audacious mouse terrorizing my apartment. But by the time I arrived with my feline assassin, the mouse had already succumbed to the square of Hershey's I had set upon a wooden trap.

Death by chocolate.

So now I have a cat and no mice.

But you're already one step ahead of me, aren't you?

Very early in the morning, three days after I brought Mimi home, I woke to find her making a little bed on my tummy. I petted her head, pleased that she had finally decided to make friends. After a few minutes, I got up in the dim blue morning light and padded barefoot across the room to the bathroom. Then I hopped back into bed, disappointed that the cat had now disappeared. I put on my glasses to check what time it was. In doing so, a small gray lump on the rug came into focus.

Another mouse.

A dead one.

Smack-dab in the middle of the path to the bathroom, and yet by some miracle, I hadn't stepped on it.

Have you ever doubted if there is a God? Well, now you know.

I woke up my boyfriend. I'm not squeamish, but there was no way I was letting him sleep through this.

Why do we have boyfriends if not to take care of dead mice?

"Wow," he said, peering over at it. "This is a clean kill!"

"Don't look at it, honey, it's sad."

His boyish enthusiasm continued. "No blood at all! She must have broken its neck with one bite."

Mimi, the hired hit cat. No pleasure, no mistakes.

My boyfriend scooped the mouse into a

trash bag and said he'd take it out.

"Wait," I said. "If you're taking it out, let me clean the litter box."

So the mouse was laid to rest, buried beneath the excrement of its killer.

I guess Mimi and I both are pretty cold.

But this early success made me cocky. A few days later, I caught sight of the varmint perched atop my dog's dish in the kitchen. We both froze. Then the mouse darted beneath my oven, a dead end.

I thought, *Where is the frigging cat?*

Only my dog sat nearby. I grabbed him, threw him into my small galley kitchen, and barricaded him inside with a wall of dining chairs. He plopped down right in front of the oven and smiled at me, tail wagging across the floor.

He was completely unaware that we had a hostage situation — and he was my gunman.

Every operation needs a dopey-but-loyal thug.

With Pip unwittingly guarding the exit, I ran in search of the cat. I looked under the couch, between the bookshelves, behind the curtains. In my closet, I army-crawled over the piles of shoes that lined the floor, I shifted all the hangers in case she had latched onto one like forgotten dry-cleaning.

Angel-faced killer

No cat.

I ran back to the kitchen and opened a can of tuna.

"Meow?" Mimi suddenly materialized behind me.

But the cat was now too distracted to notice any mouse. I scooped up the cat, threw the tuna in the fridge, and set her down in front of the oven. The mouse was still under there, cowering in the corner. I tried to draw Mimi's attention to it.

Have you ever tried directing a cat?

Then you're a step ahead of me again.

I batted a plastic tab from a milk jug around and shot it underneath the oven; Mimi sniffed the air for more tuna.

I grabbed the cat-dancer toy and made it do a jig before flicking the feathered end under the oven, like fly-fishing for mice; Mimi started cleaning her paws.

I tried to gently angle Mimi's face down to be eye level with the mouse; she took to it like a wild mustang to a halter.

I realized I had only one option left, and it was a gamble. I'd have to scare the mouse out so she would see it. Mimi Bourne could take it from there.

So I got flat on my belly, once again eye-to-beady-eye with a rodent, and I used the long stick of the cat dancer to reach the mouse.

Mind you, I would also be scaring it *toward* my face. But with my finger hooked in Mimi's collar, I knew she had my back.

I touched the mouse with the stick, the

mouse shot forward, I flew back by sheer force of terror and Mimi . . .

Mimi missed it completely. She was so freaked out by my behavior, she jumped up on the counter, out of the kitchen, and disappeared again.

So I have a cat and a mouse in my house. I just don't know where.

DR. MOTHER MARY

BY LISA

Mother Mary went to the hospital this week, where she was probably the only person admitted wearing a lab coat.

Physician, heal thyself.

You may not know that Mother Mary wears a lab coat all the time, though she's no doctor. She buys them at the Dollar Store and says she likes having all those pockets.

I'm sure that surgeons feel the same way. But who says you need a medical degree to like pockets?

Lab coats for everyone!

By the way, she's already home from the hospital, so don't worry.

I'll worry enough for both of us.

We begin the story by telling you that last week, she was fine. In fact, my brother Frank sent me a photo of them both, out to dinner. And yes, she wore her lab coat, because I don't make anything up.

I may be the author, but my family does all the writing.

The day after they sent me the photo, I called Mother Mary to say hi, and she was enjoying a visit with her speech therapist, Dorian. You may remember that she has been having speech problems since her stroke, though she still curses like a champ.

Mother Mary remains fluent in profanity.

Thank God the best swearwords are one syllable.

Anyway, that's how I know she's doing fine. If I ask her too many questions about her health, she'll tell me to go to hell.

Yay!

Anyway, Speech Therapist Dorian comes to see her three times a week, and she adores him. She always tells me how nice he is to her, and she always does her homework for him, practicing her vowel sounds from flash cards, just to make him happy.

Bottom line, Mother Mary has a crush on Speech Therapist Dorian.

It's not therapy, it's dating.

At least in her mind.

This is especially so because he's Chinese, and Mother Mary has a thing for Asian men.

Don't ask why, because I have no idea. All

I know is that she always adored my father's old college friend Pete Ong. That was sixty-odd years ago, and it never stopped. He may well have been Japanese or Korean, we'll never know, but it's all the same to her.

Pete Ong, wherever you are, call her.

It's a sure thing, if you catch my drift.

To stay on point, the first time she met Speech Therapist Dorian, she called me afterwards and told me that he was Chinese, which is either his nationality or her code for superhot.

Plus I've seen a photo of Dorian, and he is superhot.

She may be ninety, but she's still kicking.

And she may have cataracts, but she ain't blind.

In fact, she's so crazy about him that she put him on the phone with me when I called her last week. "Hi, Dorian," I said. "How's she doing?"

"Great," he answered cheerfully. "Also, she wants me to tell you I'm Chinese."

I'm not making this up, either.

This actually happened, I swear.

Mother Mary forgets I know he's Chinese, so she had to have him remind me.

Now *there's* an aspect of old age nobody ever tells you about.

You forget your fetishes.

Anyway, she was fine until one day, she told my brother Frank that some prune juice she drank "went down the wrong pipe" and now she's having trouble breathing.

Thank God, he takes her to the hospital right away, because we both know that although Dr. Mother Mary has a lab coat, she lacks the medical degree.

Or the plumbing license.

Anyway, she was admitted for observation and testing, and they found and drained some fluid from around her heart, which is no laughing matter.

We know she has heart issues, though she has more heart than anyone I've ever known.

So Brother Frank is keeping an anxious eye on her, and God bless the caregivers.

He's a great son and brother, and she couldn't be in better hands. Nor would she want to be.

Except maybe Dorian's.

I'm What's Cooking
BY LISA

This is about food.

Because I'm on a diet.

Since I can't have food, it's all I think about.

I've been working a lot and I keep the TV on in my office when I work. And everything on TV is about food.

In other words, it's TV's fault I gained a permanent ten pounds.

Half the shows on TV are cooking shows, and I watch every one of them. Rachael Ray, Anthony Bourdain, Martha Stewart, Lydia Bastianich, Mike Colameco, the Barefoot Contessa, and Nigella Lawson. Then there are cooking shows with multiple chefs, like *The Chew.* At night there so many chef shows, the chefs have to compete to stay on the shows, and if they lose, they pack their knives and go.

But not really, because there's always

another show to replace them, with cooking.

And whether it's daytime or nighttime, every talk show will have a cooking segment, so you can watch comedians and actresses whip up chicken cacciatore. They serve the audience the food, and everyone munches away while the cooking continues.

Hungry yet?

In between the cooking segments are food commercials, whether it's the latest frozen food or a Seafood Shanty, Olive Garden, McDonald's, Burger King, Carrabba's, Outback Steakhouse, or Domino's Pizza.

Yes, they deliver.

To your mouth.

And hips.

I know there are channels dedicated to round-the-clock food programming, but what I'm trying to tell you is that all of the channels are food channels. And all the food shows, restaurants, and recipes are trying to solve the problem every mom seems to have every night, which is what to have for dinner.

Let me tell you how Mother Mary solved that problem.

She made spaghetti with tomato sauce, or gravy, as everybody knows it should be called. And on the side, she served an iceberg salad dressed with oil and vinegar.

Do you understand what I'm saying? We had the same thing for dinner, every night of my life.

I'm not complaining.

Who doesn't love spaghetti?

Plus Mother Mary made the best gravy in the world. She slow-cooked a big pot of it on Sunday and parceled it out all week, over five nights of having spaghetti.

And iceberg lettuce? Love it. It's crunchy water.

Great if you're hungry. Or thirsty.

Come Saturday night we ate hoagies, pizza, or cold spaghetti.

Not kidding.

And on Sunday we had a big meal that was ravioli, with a side of spaghetti.

You know how when you're growing up you think that everything in your house is normal?

You don't even realize there is another way until you meet other people and they look at you like you're crazy?

I remember the exact moment this happened, with my friend Miriam, who came over for dinner and remarked that both times she had been over my house, we had spaghetti.

And that's when I told her that we had

spaghetti every night.

She looked at me like I was crazy.

Did she laugh? Did she bully me?

No and no.

She started coming over my house for dinner, every night.

You know why?

Because everybody loves spaghetti.

I myself could eat spaghetti every night, and probably every day for lunch, and also cold the next morning, for breakfast. It doesn't make sense to me, even now, that we change what we have for dinner.

Think about it.

Most people eat the same thing every day for breakfast — cereal, or maybe eggs.

So why would you change what you have for dinner, every day?

It creates a lot of problems, and also TV shows and channels and commercials, and unnecessary food products, and chain restaurants in strip malls, when we could all just make spaghetti, eat up, and be happy.

Buon appetito.

MOTHER MARY

BY LISA

I am very sorry to have to tell you that Mother Mary's health has taken a dramatic and unexpected turn for the worse, so this won't be funny.

Except for the fact that she is at her funniest when times are darkest.

She's been newly diagnosed with advanced lung cancer, has moved up North with me, and has entered hospice care at my house. Mercifully, Brother Frank, Daughter Francesca, and family and friends are all around her, and she is resting comfortably. So comfortably, in fact, that the hospice nurses, who are saints on wheels, cannot believe it. One nurse asked Mother Mary if she was having any pain — and she pointed to me.

So you get the idea.

She sleeps a lot, but when she is awake, she loves to have visitors. It hurts her throat to talk too much, so she writes on a wipe-off erase board, and you will be happy to know that most of what she writes is unprintable here.

Not even cancer can trump profanity.

Whatever she writes is funny and brilliant, and her mind is sharper than it's ever been. Some friends visited her yesterday, and she remembered the name of a lawyer they both knew some fifty years ago, though they could not, at a fraction of her age.

Me, I can't remember where my car keys are.

Maybe I should tell Mother Mary and she'll remind me.

Please don't think my tone herein is inappropriate. These have always been books about family, the ups and downs, the laughter and the tears, and I think it's appropriate to have both here, maybe even in the same sentence.

I would guess if you're a fan of this series, and especially of Mother Mary, you have a great sense of humor, and The Flying Scottolines have always handled disaster with humor. In fact, catastrophe is our middle name.

That's why you pronounce the final E, to make it Italian.

I also know that many of you have gone through this heartbreaking journey

yourselves. If you have, you already know that hospice plunges you into a world different from any other, filled with irony and incongruities.

You will get a delivery of a shower chair and a commode, which will be the only furniture delivery you don't get excited about.

You will open the refrigerator and it will contain potato salad and morphine. Only one of these is organic.

You will find yourself granting every wish of your mother's as if it were her last, because, well, it could be. We have all been running hither and yon getting mango sorbet, Bud Light, Entenmann's plain donuts, and mashed potatoes with gravy. I had a fight in Whole Foods over the last jar of puréed pears baby food, which was for my Mother Mary.

You haven't lived until you've bought baby food for your mother, depriving a nine-month-old.

Take that, baby. Try the carrots, you selfish little thing.

We are alternately happy and sad, getting along wonderfully or bickering. I don't worry about this. In fact, I think it's par for the course. If you're not irritable at a time like this, you lack perspective.

I never sweat the small stuff, but this is clearly not the small stuff. I've spent my life dismissing minor annoyances because they aren't a matter of life and death, but this is a matter of life and death.

Trust me, we're sweating it.

Yet we persevere, because we have no other choice and we're lucky to have this one. We ask the hospice nurses how long we will have Mother Mary with us, and one nurse says something truly profound — that people die the way they lived.

That's good news with Mother Mary.

She's a fighter and she's fighting. When the priest arrived to give her last rites, she sent him away.

Actually what she said was, "Never!"

So she is not going gentle.

She cannot spell gentle.

She even insists that I go on book tour, since I have a book out this week, and though I am torn, I will obey her. She doesn't want me to act like the end is near, or it makes her feel as if it is, and I understand that, too. So in another irony, because she comes first, I'm going to listen to her and do my job.

By the way, I showed her an advance copy of the new book that Daughter Francesca and I wrote, which is dedicated to her. She was thrilled to see it, and the book will be out in summer. I'm betting on her being with us then too.

Because here's the one thing I truly believe:

Mother Mary will be with us forever.

FEAR OF FLYING
BY LISA

Lately, I'm grabbing men on airplanes.

This could be the new match.com, for frequent flyers.

Let me explain. I have a medical excuse.

I seem to be developing a fear of flying.

And I blame Liam Neeson.

Because after seeing the movie *Nonstop,* as well as lots of other airplane crash movies, I can visualize all too well what happens when planes become lawn darts. It might be too much information, or too much imagination. Either way, all of a sudden, I'm nervous when I fly.

I found this out this week, when I took a business trip to Florida from Philly, down one day and up the next, which describes the turbulence both ways.

There had been bad rainstorms all over the country, and the plane ride south started off rocky and never got better. I popped flop sweat. I gripped the armrests. I gritted my teeth.

But when I looked around at the other passengers, they were reading their books, ebooks, and newspapers and answering email. Oddly, they seemed not to realize that the world was about to end.

The captain got on the speaker and said things like "random air pockets," "being rerouted," "keep your seat belts fastened," but I was too stressed out to hear any of it, and all I can tell you is that it was the first flight I wouldn't get up to go to the bathroom.

I almost went in my seat.

Then the plane dropped suddenly, and I instinctively reached over and clutched the arm of the man next to me.

I say instinctively, but God knows if it's instinctive.

Maybe it's instinctive for single women.

Either way, he looked over and smiled, and I apologized.

Then he said, "Don't worry. We're at thirty-five thousand feet."

Oy.

I said, "That's exactly what worries me."

He shook his head, patiently. "It shouldn't. If anything goes wrong now, the pilot has thirty thousand feet to fix it. The only times to worry are at takeoff and landing."

Yikes.

So I gutted it out, and I helped land the plane through the sheer power of will, hope, karma, prayer, or all of the above.

It took the next three hours for my stomach to settle, and I dreaded the flight home the next day, which was even worse. The sky was sunny and clear, but wind buffeted the plane, up and down, right and left, and again, when we made a sudden drop, I grabbed the guy next to me.

Are you getting the idea? Don't sit near me on a plane.

But this guy was nice, too. He laughed patiently as I apologized and unhooked my nails from his arm, one at a time like a kitten.

Then he said, "You don't have to worry. There's nothing out there."

Oy.

I told him, "That's exactly what worries me."

"It shouldn't. It means there's nothing for us to hit, or to hit us."

"But it also means there's nothing *underneath* us."

"No worries. You're in more danger on the street, with all those crazy drivers. This is nothing, and the plane's on autopilot. Do you know they don't even drive with their hands on the wheel?"

I almost threw up.

Then, by some miracle, after we landed safely, I filed weak-kneed down the aisle, where the pilot stood next to a flight attendant. I asked the pilot, "Is it true that you don't drive with your hands on the wheel?"

"No," he answered.

"Yes," answered the flight attendant, at the same time.

And I'm driving to Florida, from now on.

LOVE WITHOUT ROUGH EDGES

BY FRANCESCA

During most of grandmother's time in hospice, I was sitting only a few feet from her. I tried to help however I could and keep her company the rest of the time. But hospice is a game you play to lose, and it was difficult to adjust.

Often, I felt helpless.

So when my uncle said that my grandmother had specifically asked for me to do her nails, I was elated — unlike the daunting medical side of hospice, this was something I knew I could handle.

My grandmother took meticulous care of her fingernails. She always carried an emery board in her handbag, and even when her knuckles knotted with arthritis, she kept each filed to a perfect almond shape.

Even now, she could feel her nails were long, but she couldn't feel the advanced cancer in her chest.

One of many blessings.

So I was happy to help. I envisioned giving her a salon experience, complete with soaking bowls of warm, sudsy water and a hand massage with scented lotion. I wanted so badly to do something nice for her, something special.

When you know that anything could be the last something, you want everything to be perfect.

But the next morning, I could see she was exhausted, more so than the day before.

It takes a lot for a body to launch a spirit. Especially one like hers.

I put my hand on her shoulder as she napped on the couch. "Is it all right if I do your nails while you rest?"

She opened her eyes for a moment and gave a nod.

I took her hands one by one, my fingers threaded through hers. I filed each nail gently, so as not to disturb her, rounding the tips into half-moons. I ran my fingers over them to make sure they were perfectly clean and smooth, no rough edges.

I thought of all that those hands had done in ninety years. Before my time, she was a songwriter, her hands played many melodies on piano. I imagined her penciling in the margins of a new song, adding dynamic changes, a *ritardando* at the end.

If only there was a *ritardando* in real life. But you can't hold on to one minute longer than any other. And the more you try, the faster the minutes seem to go.

I thought of all that those hands had done for me. How many meals had they prepared? How many other babysitters served homemade ravioli as an afterschool snack? How many times had they stroked my hair? Touched my cheek? How many gestures of

April Narby

love can a lifetime hold?

In my grandmother's case, countless.

So I held on to her hands while she slept. And I whispered to her, told her things, some important and some mundane, some I'd said a thousand times before, some I'd never said 'til then.

I hoped she could feel in my hands the love returned to her, the lessons learned, the strength she'd instilled in me now trying to be strong for her.

I always admired my grandmother's combination of grit and warmth, she could be tough and tender, hard and soft.

Although she was all soft with me.

She loved without rough edges.

After some time she woke up, or maybe she hadn't been asleep at all, and she ran her thumb over her fingertips. She smiled. "Good," she told me, and she blew me a kiss.

I wondered if she had heard me say that I loved her enough to hope she could let go.

Even though I wanted to hold her hands a while longer.

MOTHER MARY AND FRANK SINATRA

BY LISA

I'm sorry to have to write that Mother Mary has passed, and we are all deeply, profoundly shocked and heartbroken.

I don't want this to veer into the maudlin, so I won't elaborate on our emotions. You know them if you've been there, or if you have a heart.

But permit me to say one last thing on the subject.

It's my last word.

On her last words.

Let me begin by saying that all of us, including my mother, were surprised when we found out she had late-stage lung cancer and that her death was imminent. Her kind pulmonologist explained it all to her carefully, so she knew the end was near. But another doctor happened to mention the term "end-of-life" care, which went over like a lead balloon, one of Mother Mary's favorite expressions. When we got home, her throat hurt too much to talk, so we got her a Sharpie and dry-erase board, and the first thing she wrote, in large letters, was: DON'T SAY ANYTHING ABOUT END OF LIFE AROUND HERE.

So we didn't.

And when a visitor asked her how she was feeling, she wrote, OUTSIDE OF ALL THIS CRAP, I'M DOING FINE.

And to one of her friends, Nino, she wrote, SEE YOU IN THE SUMMER.

Secretly, I kept wondering if she was in denial about her own death. I'm a bookish sort, so I read the pamphlet they gave us from hospice, which advised that the terminally ill often want to talk with loved ones about the important events of their lives, offer them parting gifts or mementos, or say good-bye in a variety of other ways.

Mother Mary did none of these things.

She hadn't read the pamphlet.

And even so, she wasn't the type of woman to do anything by the book.

During her last few days, I used to lie awake at night, worrying that she wasn't going to have the typical, or normal, death, whatever that is. We weren't going to say good-bye, like in the pamphlets or the movies. I was fine with that, but I worried that if she didn't accept her own death, would

April Narby

she be fearful when it came?

Thankfully, no, she wasn't.

She was dozing, under a dose of morphine that eased her pain but not her senses. She squeezed my brother's hand one last time, three squeezes that were her signal for I Love You.

Those were her last words.

In retrospect, I realize that Mother Mary knew she was ill, but she wasn't ready to accept death, offer us mementos, or say good-bye.

Why?

Because she had hope.

And she kept that alive.

And in return, hope kept her alive, for much longer than the doctors expected.

She didn't provide us the storybook final scene as she passed from this earth, but it

April Narby

Mother Mary did it her way and always kept us laughing.

wasn't supposed to be about our comfort. It wasn't about us at all, or the pamphlets or the movies.

It was about her, and she faced death the way she confronted life — on her terms.

It won't surprise you to know that her favorite singer was Frank Sinatra and her favorite song, "My Way."

In all things, she did it her way.

She wouldn't concede to cancer. The only way it would win was to beat her, and in the end, she still won.

Disease took her body, but not her soul.

Her spirit was full of hope and life.

Her last words were about love.

This will be my last word on the sadness and grief on the subject of her passing. From now on, I choose to write about her the way we all knew her — funny, strong, sassy, and full of life. Francesca and I have received an incredible outpouring of sympathy cards, emails, Facebook posts, and donations, and it's a comfort to see that many of our readers loved Mother Mary and saw their own mothers in her, through the stories that Francesca and I wrote about her. We are overwhelmed with gratitude by them, as Mother Mary would be. It's testament to the kindness of our readers, as well as to the power of books.

And I promise there will be more Mother Mary stories, because she was full of surprises. After all, it was only recently that I discovered her real name was Maria, not Mary.

So stay tuned and see what's in store.

In the end, Mother Mary will get the last laugh.

WHO NEEDS IT?

BY FRANCESCA

Sometimes life throws you too much to process at once. After I broke up with my boyfriend of two years, I barely had enough time to tell my friends when, just five days later, my mom called me to say that my grandmother, Mother Mary, was being hospitalized in Pennsylvania. I left my apartment and went home that day.

At first I didn't know how bad things were; none of us did. In the waiting room at the ER, my uncle and I caught up casually, and I mentioned the breakup.

"Don't tell Mom, okay?" my uncle requested. "I don't want her to hear anything to upset her."

I frowned. I didn't agree the news would disappoint my grandmother; she had liked my boyfriend, but she wasn't so traditional as to fret over my marriage prospects. As a two-time divorcée herself, she had excellent perspective on romantic woes.

But at that moment the doctor called us in with the results of her CAT scan and radiographs, and then I remember him saying those words that blot out other thought:

Lung cancer. Metastasized. Advanced.

And those that still echo the loudest: "a matter of weeks."

The rest of her life measured in weeks. It seemed absurd.

It was impossible to process.

My grandmother, however, was just happy the doctors said she could go home.

While the three of us cared for her at my mother's house, my grandmother handled everything with grace and her characteristic humor, but little sentimentality. We were given a pamphlet that encouraged hospice caregivers to reminisce with their loved ones and ask for stories of the past. But my grandmother would have none of it.

She didn't want to look at old photo albums, and she didn't want to say anything approaching a goodbye. She refused to lie in a bed, so instead we set up camp on the couch.

But our family is Italian, so trying to get our relatives to tone down their emotions was a different story. For them, overcooking the eggplant is reason enough for tears. Learning our matriarch was in hospice called for opera.

So our family members visiting from South Philly were crying before we opened the door. But then, so were we.

Seeing relatives file in made it real; they were coming to say goodbye.

I busied myself with the trays of food — of course, we had food — so that they'd have some time alone with my grandmother.

Imagine my surprise when a few minutes later, I heard laughter. I brought in the tray of snacks.

"Look what she wrote!" Aunt Nana said when I came in. She held up my grandmother's whiteboard:

"Did you bring the Dago red?" — slang for homemade Italian wine. Then my grandmother snatched it back, and added, "I'll give you $100 for two quarts."

Her messages were so charming and funny, my family started taking pictures of them. That set off my grandmother's maudlin-meter, so her messages got increasingly profane.

I now have Kodak moments of my relatives holding signs with messages of hope, such as: "Eat Shit."

Suitable for framing.

My grandmother entertained our extended family for several hours, holding court the way she always did. As they were leaving, one relative jokingly scolded us for "scaring" them by saying she was close to the end, when she "clearly" had plenty more time.

She didn't.

Her decline happened whether we were ready for it or not. My grandmother soon became too tired for many visitors. Her waking hours became fewer. Her handwriting on the whiteboard became more slanting and wiggly. Her speech became very difficult.

Though I could usually understand.

One day, my mom convinced my uncle to get out of the house with her, and I took care of my grandmother by myself. She wanted to nap on the couch with the television on and her feet in my lap, and I was more than happy to oblige. I was thrilled to know what exactly she wanted and to be able to do it, for a change. So, I sat still as a statue, as she slept to the lullaby of her favorite shows — *Judge Alex, Judge Judy, Divorce Court.*

I must say, *Divorce Court* is an excellent program.

When she woke, I prepared a balanced lunch of her specific request: lukewarm coffee, Sprite, light beer, Milano cookies, and a variety of sorbets.

We were rocking hospice.

After lunch, she wanted to sit up for a while. I wanted to give her a conversational break from answering the same questions about her health: Are you okay? Are you hungry? Are you thirsty? Do you have to go to the bathroom? She was ailing, I knew, but she was still in there.

And knowing her as I do, I thought she might be bored.

But the only thing non-hospice related that I could come up with was my breakup. Not because I wanted to unburden myself — any part of my life a few weeks ago seemed miles and miles away — but I wanted to talk to her without taxing her.

So I commenced a monologue. I didn't know if she was listening, but occasionally she would nod, so I barreled on. I explained the lead-up to the breakup, the first signs of trouble, the ways I tried to fix it, the ways it couldn't be fixed, the things I'll miss most, the things I did wrong, and what I'll try to do better next time.

I was rambling.

Until my grandmother stopped me and motioned for her whiteboard. I held it steady for her while she inscribed, slow enough to build suspense:

"Motto — Who Needs It???"

Then she burst out laughing, which made me crack up, and we both dissolved into a fit of giggles.

Who needs it? In other words, *enough, let it go, next.*

Toward the end of my relationship with my boyfriend, I had been consumed with considering every angle of interpretation, every possible misstep I might have taken, every potential outcome that didn't come true. But with one simple phrase, my grandmother had offered an instant dose of perspective.

Perspective doesn't mean seeing all; it means seeing what matters.

My grandmother had never been the most reflective person. She couldn't afford to be. Growing up in very difficult circumstances taught — or forced — her to act instead of ponder, to escape instead of fix, and to move on instead of regret. This may not be the perfect way to live, but it was the only way she could survive.

I grew up the child of several troubled marriages. I am the watcher, the thinker, the healer. I read people, I adapt, I fix — or try to. And if it fails, I stew on all the ways it could've gone differently. This is not always a bad way to be.

But it's not always good.

Bad things happen, and dwelling about how they're bad, why they're bad, doesn't make them any better. Sometimes you need to ask yourself, "Who needs it?" Evaluate your present, not only your past. See if what you're doing to yourself is helping you. If the answer is no, then "Who needs it?" Let it go.

There were so many times before that day that I worried that my grandmother wasn't having the best hospice experience, although I had no idea what that might be. When my grandmother rejected the sentimental stuff, the nostalgia, the goodbyes, I feared we weren't creating the right environment or supporting her correctly so that she could process and make peace with what was happening.

But who needs it?

My grandmother didn't waste her last days looking backwards. There was nothing that needed processing. Life happens, whether we approve it or not. Instead, she chose to live in the moment, to savor, to laugh, to enjoy those around her.

This was the way she lived, and the way she died, and it was the wisdom I most needed to hear from the only woman who could give it.

Rollin' On

BY LISA

The great thing about friends is that sometimes they realize what you need even before you do.

For example, my bestie Laura gave me a bicycle last Christmas, and I thought it was a really cool gift. But I hadn't ridden a bicycle in about three hundred years, and this bike had so many bells and whistles that I didn't know if I'd ever figure it out.

Plus no kickstand.

I mean really.

I wrote about the bike but worried that might be the most use I got out of it.

Once again, I was wrong.

It was a beautiful Saturday in spring, after Mother Mary had passed, and I was looking for ways to distract and/or amuse myself.

Grief is a funny thing, it settles into your bones like a dormant virus and becomes a part of you, lying in wait to flare up. Most of the time, it behaves itself, but sometimes it doesn't, and I found that keeping myself busy works wonders.

I know this isn't a new idea, that's the kind of girl I am. I reinvent the wheel, every time.

I was about to work on my next book, but on impulse, I turned to the bike. I didn't really know where to ride it, and there are way too many hills in my neighborhood.

I'm looking for distraction, not a cardiac.

So I threw it in the back of the car, drove to the park, spotted a bike trail, and hopped on. True, I couldn't figure out the gears, but it turned out not to matter, because whatever gear it came in was great, and in a matter of minutes, I had joined a flock of noisy and unruly eleven-year-olds on the bike path.

Not that I'm complaining.

There's nothing like a group of giggling kids to lift your mood, especially when they're somebody else's.

Also I got to ride behind them, acting like I was being a considerate adult, instead of an immediately exhausted one.

Meanwhile, the trail was beautiful, with the trees budding green, the baby birds chirping, and the smooth asphalt making a path for the menopausal.

Nature has its limits. If you can pave

something to make it easier on your knees, fine by me.

Surprisingly, you really don't forget how to ride a bike, and I began to enjoy the sensation of the sun on my SPF and the balmy breezes cooling my sweaty armpits.

I'm a poet, right?

I let my thoughts run free, and happily they didn't return to anything morbid, but rather my brain seemed to empty out, an altogether pleasant sensation.

I think this is called relaxation, but I'm not sure.

I'm a relaxation virgin.

And then I realized that I was having fun, all by myself except for the laughing kids, and in time I felt eleven years old myself.

The kids had fun pretending to swerve their bikes into each other, and I wondered if they would be friends five years later, or ten, or even twenty, like Laura and me. I thought of Franca, Sandy, and Rachel, my friends of forty years' standing, who have been so wonderful to me about Mother Mary's passing. I even have friends like Nan and Paula, whom I've been close to for fifteen years, which qualifies them as new friends.

How lucky am I, in these loyal friends?

How lucky are you, in yours?

Keep pedaling, my friend.

Life is a bike path through the woods, generally smooth, but not without its bumps and turns.

Hang on.

And ride together.

Laughing.

WE KNEW YOU WOULDN'T AMOUNT TO ANYTHING

BY LISA

I'll never forget the day my high school guidance counselor told me I was an overachiever.

I said, thank you.

Then I went home and looked it up.

Since then, "overachiever" has become one of my favorite words of all time.

I like its honesty.

It means, none of us thought you would amount to anything, but it turns out that you can walk and chew gum at the same time.

Can you think of a better insult-compliment?

Really, you're doing a lot better than anybody thought you would with what God gave you. Will wonders never cease?

By the way, when I say I went home and looked it up, I looked it up in something we used to have in the olden days, called a dictionary. This was a big thick book, from when we used to have books. The pages of a dictionary were thin and crinkly, and there were little black half wells in the side for your finger, which provided hours of enjoyment in ancient times, back when there were kickstands on bicycles.

Did I mention that my bicycle doesn't have a kickstand, either?

Why there are no more kickstands on bicycles is a complete mystery to me. A kickstand is one of the most useful things ever in the whole wide world, and now I have to lean my new bicycle against the wall instead of having it stand up all by itself.

Why?

I see nothing wrong with having a kickstand on a bike. In fact, I wish I had a kickstand on my body.

I can't tell you the number of times I'm in a conversation with someone and I think, I'm going to lean against the wall while we have this conversation, because it's taking a long time and I don't want to have to hold myself up.

But I digress.

I am an overachiever, so it follows naturally that I would overdo things.

One of the things I'm overdoing is over-improving my home.

I also love the word "over-improving."

It's another great insult-compliment, isn't it?

In other words, you're fixing up your house, but none of us thinks you'll ever get the money back for it. We knew you'd do something stupid eventually and now you've gone and done it. You haven't improved the kitchen or the bathroom, which are the two places that everybody knows increase the value of your home. So, as we predicted all along, you're blowing your hard-earned money on dumb stuff, which makes a lot of sense to us, though we never thought you'd make any money in the first place. It figures that you'd make it writing books, since the only people who buy books are the people who like dictionaries, and we all know how plentiful they are nowadays.

Like that.

Okay, so let me tell you about the dumb thing I'm doing, which is putting on a room. I don't know what the room is called but I can tell you how it came about. I love being outside in my backyard, playing with the dogs, reading, or writing by squinting at the laptop in the sun. I'd been thinking a lot to myself that it would be great to have a room that I could work in and be sort-of inside and sort-of outside, to save myself from squinting, which as we all know gives you wrinkles and I have plenty of those.

I told this idea to someone and she said, you mean a "three-season room."

This term appealed to me instantly, as it sounded exactly like the kind of thing an overachiever would do, spend money to make a room that you can only live in for three seasons.

Also it sounded better than that no-squinting room.

Or wrinkle-free room.

So they're building my three-season room right now, and it has windows on three sides, with a flagstone floor, and I can't wait until it's finished, so I can go inside and sit around with the dogs.

And overachieve.

Because it doesn't matter what anybody else thinks you can do, only what you think you can do.

Ha!

Know what that was?

The last laugh.

HARDBALL AT THE GYM
BY FRANCESCA

After my breakup, I recommitted myself to fitness. I had a case of long-term-relationship body, a "my best angle is your love" situation, and I needed to get back to "howdy, stranger."

I also recently learned that loyalty's got nothing over shiny and new.

My ex-boyfriend didn't teach me that, my gym did.

My gym and I have been seeing each other, off-and-on, for five years. I didn't want to break up, I only wanted to change locations within the same company, but my gym is unsupportive.

If I were a new member looking to join, the gym would waive more than half the initiation fee. But for a lousy old member, simply switching locations slaps me with a "transfer fee" that exceeds the initiation offer by $150!

I should've known. This gym and I have

baggage.

When I first joined in 2009, I wanted the most basic membership. But I was informed that I had to buy the most expensive option, the "All-Access Pass," which afforded me admittance to any of the chain's gyms in the country, for a much less affordable price.

"It's a required upgrade," the consultant explained, as if that were an explanation.

Isn't an upgrade, by definition, optional?

"Normally yes, but this is a Flagship location."

A red flagship.

Fast-forward five years, I've moved farther from my old gym and closer to a newer location — and this one has a rooftop pool!

Finally, I'd be able to get some of the perk I've been paying for since 2009, right?

"I'm sorry," the guy told me when I tried to check in last month. "This gym is excluded from All-Access."

Uh, you've been charging me for "All-Access," not "Some-Access."

"You need an upgrade for Destination locations like this one."

Even if the destination is four blocks away?

I explained that while I understood he doesn't make the rules, the rules are really stupid.

He glanced over his shoulder and leaned in. "Look, I hear you. You can skip the upgrade and join only this location. It'll even be cheaper than All-Access."

Where do I sign?

Then he added, "Are you familiar with our transfer fee?" and introduced me to my new arbitrary charge.

Hello, Transfer Fee? Meet Sucker.

As much as I wanted in, I couldn't accept their gouging. I left to think about it.

Read, stew about it.

I was determined to get out of the fee. I tallied up how much I had spent as a five-year member, a sum I'm too ashamed to print, because for that price, I should be so much hotter.

It was during my online research that I discovered the new-member promotion. I thought there was no way they could justify rewarding the newbies while punishing the faithful. I was sure I'd persuade them to waive the transfer or at least meet the new member price. I called to make my case.

I tried honey, I tried vinegar, appeals to logic and emotion.

He shot down every argument.

I said I'd cancel at my old location and re-up with him as a new member.

"If you cancel, you stay in our system for

three months, so you'd miss the whole summer."

He had the pool card, and he knew it.

Despite my indignation, I knew that by not joining this gym, I'd be cutting off my nose to spite my face.

Or keeping my fat to spite my thighs.

I conceded, my credit-card information tasting bitter on my tongue.

Don't get mad, get even. To stick it to them, I go to the gym every day, front and center at all the classes, and I use a vindictive amount of free conditioner in the showers.

My hate-workouts are paying off. I've lost seven pounds.

Shiny and new, here I come.

CREDIT WHERE CREDIT IS DUE

BY LISA

I just came back from New York City and I learned an important life lesson, but not until I got home.

Let me explain.

I was in New York for Book Expo, which is a book trade show for authors, agents, publishers, librarians, and booksellers. It's totally fun, and I love to go, not only because I love book people, but because I get to see an agent who rejected me a long time ago, when I was looking for a publisher. I'll never forget his rejection letter, which read, "We don't have time to take any new clients and if we did, we wouldn't take you."

I've held a grudge against him for twenty-five years, because Mother Mary taught me to keep hate alive.

Unfortunately, I didn't get to see him at Book Expo, and I'm hoping he's dead.

Too dark?

And even if he is, I still hate him.

That's how good at hating Mother Mary taught me to be, and believe me, if she were still alive, she would want him dead, too.

To come to my point, I went to Book Expo with Daughter Francesca to promote our book *Have a Nice Guilt Trip.* This was the first time that Francesca and I had promoted a book together at Book Expo. I just happened to be standing on the trade-show floor, but at a distance, when she got recognized by some wonderful librarians who were walking behind her, but in front of me.

I overheard one of them say, "I think that's Francesca Serritella, who writes those funny books with her mother. My daughter loves her writing."

It was a lovely thing to hear, and Francesca must have heard it too, because she turned around, smiled, and introduced herself to the librarians, thanking them for their support with a hug.

I had a heart attack, but in a good way.

Happiness and pride attacked my heart, causing it to explode with Crestor and estrogen.

Okay, just Crestor.

For me, estrogen is a thing of the past.

Like sex.

In any event, what happened next was that

Francesca introduced me to the librarians, and we all hugged each other, making happy noises about mothers, daughters, and books, which is the girl trifecta.

And one of the librarians said, "Francesca is her mother's daughter, isn't she?"

April Narby
I'm amazed by both!

To which I replied, "I can't take any of the credit."

Which is what I believe.

But I didn't realize why until I left Francesca in New York and came home, where I got out of the car and the first thing I saw was my garden.

You may remember that I started a garden last year, and I planted a zillion perennials, making every rookie mistake in the book — placing plants too close together, digging too deep, putting the plants that needed sun in the shade, or watering everything so much that I broke an underground water pipe and had to have the whole lawn excavated to install a new pipe.

I have a gangrene thumb.

But when I got home, I was astounded to see that while I was away, the plants had sprung up out of nowhere and burst into glorious bloom. The phlox had vivid pink flowers, the catmint smelled minty, and the purple coneflower opened up their spiky faces. Red and yellow roses scented the air like perfume, and the sun shone so prettily on the flowers that I had to take a picture.

In the photo, you can see the sun rays, and honestly, it looks like God himself.

Nobody can take credit for a perennial garden, because we're not the gardener.

He is.
And that's true of daughters, too.

GUILT TRIPPING AT 65 MPH

BY FRANCESCA

My mom trusts me to coauthor a series of books, but she doesn't trust me to drive.

And she might be right.

We went to the Nantucket Book Festival on tour for *Have a Nice Guilt Trip,* our fifth book. I feel like our working partnership is better than ever. We've gained an easy rhythm at our speaking engagements.

We trust each other.

Just not in the car.

I realized this on the drive home from Nantucket. We couldn't stay for the whole weekend, because my mom is on deadline crunch, so we arrived on Friday and were driving back to my apartment on Saturday night. Everything was fine until darkness fell on I-95. We were in Rhode Island when I felt my mother riding the brakes.

I looked over at her. "Everything okay?"

"Yup." She was white-knuckling the wheel. The speedometer needle hovered around

40 mph. Cars and trucks were whizzing by us on both sides, several honked in frustration.

"The speed limit is sixty-five."

"I'm not gonna drive like a maniac and get us killed, okay? It doesn't matter if we go a little slower."

"Actually, with almost two hundred miles to go, a five-or ten-mile-per-hour difference really adds up. Forty miles an hour is going to take five hours, whereas sixty will take —"

"I'M DRIVING HERE."

Every daughter knows when she's pushing it, so I shut up. An hour passed, and my mom was so tense, we drove in uncharacteristic silence. It was only 10:00 P.M. but she started talking about stopping at a motel for the night.

I sighed.

"So you're going to guilt me?" she said.

"Ohmigod, I *breathed.*"

Sure, I was thinking that we could have spent the evening on Nantucket, eating lobster rolls by the sea before going to bed in the clean, crisp linens of our charming B&B. Instead, we were making our second seven-hour drive in twenty-four hours, posing a traffic hazard in the middle of I-95, and looking for a Ramada Inn.

153

But my sigh was totally innocent.

Then I had a better idea than passive-aggressive respiration: "Do you want me to drive?"

My mom took her eyes off the road to look at me, aghast.

To be fair, this wasn't an overreaction. I've been living in New York for five years, and I haven't driven regularly since I was a teenager. The last time I had to parallel-park was my driver's test.

But driving is like riding a bike, right?

A three thousand-pound, four hundred-horsepower, steel bike.

We discussed it at a rest stop. Seeing the stress on my mother's face in the fluorescent lights, I understood it didn't matter why she felt uncomfortable driving at night, only that she did. I could be more sympathetic, or, better, I could help.

She was still skeptical. "You're sure you can do this?"

"Please," I said with more confidence than I felt, "I'm almost thirty."

So we swapped seats and set out. At first, she wouldn't stop telling me to slow down, even though I was going the limit.

"Mom," I said. "I'm the captain now."

From there, we bombed home. I pushed through my fear and ignored my mother bracing against the window and the dash. I didn't know it, but she had her eyes closed for the tricky exit-jumping required to enter Manhattan.

No wonder she was no help reading the GPS.

Toward the end, a Bentley driver flagged me down, asking for directions into the city.

For the money, you'd think a Bentley would know.

I told them and offered that they could follow me.

My mom took a break from being terrified to be impressed.

Somehow, we made it safely home. I felt a greater sense of accomplishment after I parallel-parked than I did after speaking in front of one hundred people.

Out on the sidewalk, as soon as my mom got her land legs, she delivered one of her body-shaking high fives and a giant hug.

Yeah, we make a good team.

Hissy Fit Bit

BY LISA

I'm in love.

With my Fitbit.

I'm smitten, which makes me Smitbit.

Or maybe Fitbitten.

Either way, I'm into it.

If you don't know what a Fitbit is, let me explain.

It's a harmless-looking rubber band that comes in cute colors, fits around your wrist, and tracks your activity during the day. In other words, it can tell in real time whether you have been sitting on your butt like me or whether you have been engaging in something called exercise.

It doesn't know if you've been naughty or nice.

But it does see you when you're sleeping.

You can wear it to bed, and it can even track your sleep and tell you when you're restless.

Restless is code for got-up-and-went-to-the-bathroom.

The Fitbit comes preset with goals, like for example ten thousand steps, and when you've walked ten thousand steps a day, it vibrates.

Think of it as a vibrator with a PG rating.

In other words, a lousy vibrator.

My Fitbit is hot pink, and I got it as a gift from my best friend Franca, who reaches ten thousand steps by seven o'clock in the morning because she's a runner.

You could reach ten thousand steps by making 627 trips to the refrigerator, but that would not be in the spirit of Fitbithood.

Okay, I admit I did that on the first day, but not the second. Because what started to happen is that I did more activities so I could get credit from my Fitbit.

I wanted my Fitbit to approve of me.

I'm not only a people pleaser, I'm an inanimate-object pleaser.

Yes, to gain my Fitbit's love, I actually engaged in exercise. I rode my bicycle for six miles and walked the dogs for two miles.

By the way, my dogs do not have Fitbits.

They don't Fitbite.

And after my exercise, I raced home, hurried to my desk, and synced up my Fitbit with the computer, which is one of Fitbit's features. All of a sudden, pretty colored banners started flying across my monitor screen, reading HOORAY, LISA!

I got all excited!

Who doesn't need positive reinforcement in life?

After eight hours of sitting on my butt and writing, my computer never tells me, HOORAY, LISA!

But somebody pays me to write, so I'm not complaining.

HOORAY, MONEY!

By the way, the Fitbit computer display can also tell you how many calories you burn a day, but I don't look.

I want to keep the romance alive.

HOORAY IN GENERAL!

Also I don't need a bracelet to tell me I should lose weight.

I have a mirror for that.

And there's a reason nobody's making a mirror that straps to your wrist.

Another Fitbit feature I ignore is that you can connect online with other people who have Fitbit, called your Fitbit Friends, and this will enable them to see your activity levels.

I don't want Fitbit Friends.

Anybody who wants to know how many steps I walk a day isn't anybody I want to know.

If you follow.

You can even buy a Fitbit scale, which will connect wirelessly to your Fitbit bracelet and a fitness app on your phone, so that all of the inanimate objects you own can talk about how fat you are behind your back.

Needless to say, I declined.

But in no time at all, I was wearing my Fitbit every day, doing as much activity as I could, and checking my progress every night on the computer. Banners flew, badges were awarded, and my spirits soared.

GO, LISA, GO!

I actually lost a pound without meaning to, which has never happened in my life and might in fact be a typographical error.

But then one morning, I tapped my Fitbit to wake it up and it wouldn't wake up. I tried recharging it, resetting it, and doing everything I could, but it was dead. I went to the troubleshooting section of the Fitbit website, and if you've ever been to the troubleshooting section of any website, you know what happens.

You want to troubleshoot yourself.

That was a week ago, and without Fitbit to clap for me, I'm riding my bike less and barely walking the dogs at all.

I gained my pound back.

My world went from hot pink to blue.

The solution?

I might be crazy, but I'm going to buy a new one.

I know I can love again.

Can You Keep a Secret?

BY FRANCESCA

I'm keeping a secret from my best friend.

This won't be published until after the secret is out, but as I write this, I'm in the midst.

It's terrible.

No, sorry, keeping the secret is terrible. The news is wonderful:

Her boyfriend is going to propose.

"Please keep the following completely secret," began his email to me last week. I opened the attachments on my iPhone and was temporarily blinded by the photos of drop-dead-gorgeous diamond rings.

My first reaction was pure joy. I love her current boyfriend as a person and I love how he treats my friend; she's never been happier since they got together, so I was positive the "yes" was a lock.

But my elation curdled to anxiety when I realized he wasn't just letting me in on a fun secret, he was asking for advice on her favorite style, setting, cut, size, etc.

And I drew a blank. In our decade of friendship, I thought we'd discussed every topic on earth, twice. We love hypotheticals. I know which type of professional athlete she thinks would make the best husband (tennis pro), her top three cities to raise children (Providence, New York, Boston), and the breed of dog she would get (Bichon Frisé) if she liked dogs, which she doesn't.

Yet somehow, we hadn't discussed hypothetical engagement rings.

And now I'd discovered this glaring error in my best-friend duties too late. How had I not anticipated this scenario? As her in-case-of-romantic-emergency contact, I should have this information!

What if I pick something she hates and she has to wear it for the rest of her life? Could we even be friends anymore?

I'd definitely get cut from the bridesmaids roster.

If she even gets married, that is. What if I pick an ugly ring and she blames *him* for it, thus mistakenly believing that the love of her life doesn't "get" her? And it's all my fault!

It suddenly felt like I was the one proposing. Our entire relationship and future happiness were riding on this question!

Clammy hands on my keyboard, I did my best to answer each of her hopeful fiancé's questions. There was only one area I felt confident about — carat size. He suggested several options to me, but expressed concern my friend would find them "too flashy."

Oh yeah, women hate flashy diamonds.

After I'd written an appropriately tasteful preamble about how they were all gorgeous and how my friend is so in love with him she'd say yes to a shoestring, I was unequivocal: "Bigger is better. It's a no-brainer."

Just in case my friend ever saw this email exchange, I wanted her to know I had her back.

The only conversation I did remember having with my friend was about how the real charm of an engagement ring lies in imagining the man you love most in the world taking the time and care to choose a ring that shows that love returned.

So I told him not to worry about it.

However, I was worried about it.

The email was just the beginning. I pride myself on being an absolute vault when it comes to secrets, and my friends can vouch for that. But that's just it: I keep secrets *for* my friends, not *from* them, especially not my best girl.

Our friendship is defined by the telling of secrets, not the keeping of them. It's a closed circuit, so no one else is included or exposed, but between the two of us, stories, chatter, news, and gossip constantly flow.

Telling me this secret was like asking me to blow-dry my hair in the bathtub without getting shocked.

And she isn't making it easy on me.

A few days after I'd responded to her boyfriend, my friend happened to email me about celebrity engagement rings, specifically Mary-Kate Olsen's unusual vintage Cartier ring. We talk about dumb celebrity news all the time, but now this was loaded.

I needed insight into her preferences, but I was terrified of being too obvious and revealing too much. "It's cool, but also a little out there. It looks like it would get caught on sweaters. Do you like it?"

She replied within minutes, as usual.

Our BFF emails are High Priority.

She wrote, "At first I was like, what is this weird ring? But then I realized it is so Elizabeth Taylor and awesome!"

Okay, got it: weird is good, assuming it's "Elizabeth Taylor" weird.

Wait, I don't get it.

Then she forwarded a slide-show of

celebrity engagement rings, again asking my opinion while offering none of her own.

I sensed this was my last chance. I drafted my reply three times to calculate a casual tone:

"Angelina's is amazing with the emerald cuts smushed together, but do you think emerald looks as good in solitaire? I tend to like the simpler ones, like Keira Knightley's classic solitaire. But it's like, how much do you personally care about having a ring that no one else has?"

She replied, "I don't care about having a super unique ring, but I like the THOUGHT that comes with it."

The thought *I* was supposed to be thinking!

Then she moved on to speculating on what happened between Beyoncé, Solange, and Jay-Z in that elevator, and I was safe.

Beyoncé makes everything better.

I considered forwarding the whole thread to her boyfriend, but since she didn't answer any of my specific questions, I feared it would only confuse him like it had confused me. I had failed at the recon mission.

Maybe I'm not cut out for the CIA.

That said, I'm no dummy. My girlfriend-Spidey-sense guessed that the "coincidental" timing of her interest in celebrity rings might have been her testing me. So far, I'd passed. But I had no idea how I'd hold up in person.

So I avoided her.

For two weeks — a lifetime in our friendship. I didn't want to spill the beans, but I also decided that I would not lie to her. When we finally did get together for lunch, I could tell something was up.

She told me that her boyfriend recently asked her about her ring preference, completely hypothetically.

"Ohmigod! Do you think he's going to propose?" My feigned surprise was less Lee Strasberg and more Lucille Ball.

"He said sometime 'in the next five years.' "

I gulped my iced tea. I definitely couldn't keep this secret that long.

"But I think he's trying to throw me off the scent. I know he went to Tiffany's because he showed me some pictures of rings, and I have to ask . . ."

My heart thundered in my chest.

". . . is it your hand in the pictures?"

"What? No!" I squeaked. I thought fast. "Tiffany's isn't ready for these Nicki Minaj nails." I flashed my trashy bubble-gum manicure as evidence.

My friend's eyes narrowed. "Really? I'm

shocked. I was sure he'd asked you for help."

A bead of sweat formed at my temple, but I still managed to avoid perjuring myself: "It's not my hand in the picture."

I'm not the daughter of two lawyers for nothing.

Then I saw my opening: "But now that you mention it, he might ask me for help. So you should tell me *exactly what you want.*"

She did so, and I was relieved that her preferences were perfectly in line with my recommendations to her boyfriend, soon-to-be fiancé.

I was riding high. All the possible crises had been averted. She wanted to marry the boy, she was sure to get her dream ring, and I would go on record as being a great friend.

But I got cocky.

As I said goodbye to her, I asked, "If he *had* asked me for help but had sworn me to secrecy, would you have wanted me to tell you?"

She paused for a minute, then laughed. "Yeah, definitely. I'd want to know."

Grateful for my polarized sunglasses, I said goodbye and ran away.

Thankfully, her boyfriend didn't wait five years. I only had to sweat it out another month before he popped the question in Hawaii. My friend came home blessed-out and in love with her ring — and her new fiancé, of course. I was fully prepared to take the secret of my input to the grave, but her fiancé had a different idea.

"And he told me how you helped him so much!" my friend said. "He said he couldn't have done it without you."

He absolutely could have. But I'm glad I earned his trust by keeping his secret, and I'm touched that he gave me any credit at all.

He's going to be a wonderful best-friend-in-law.

My TV Is Smarter Than Your Honor Student

BY LISA

I recently converted to a smartphone, only to find out that I needed a smart TV.

D'oh!

If you recall, I wrote a few years ago about my love affair with my big TV, which at forty-two inches, took up my entire living room.

Not that I was complaining.

I loved its gargantuan screen, which made footballs look as big as watermelons and bachelorettes' heads the size of hot-air balloons.

Maybe because their heads were full of hot air.

But now my big TV looks tiny, since now there are forty-seven inches, fifty-four inches, and even larger TVs, at a fraction of the price that mine cost.

Yet I remained loyal to my big TV.

I want one marriage that lasts.

I hadn't even heard of such a thing as a

smart TV until somebody mentioned it to me, and I thought they were kidding, then when my other TV died, I replaced it with a smart TV.

I admit, I don't even know what that meant when I bought it. All I knew was that the price was right, and that they weren't charging extra for its brainpower.

So I got it home and right off the bat, I knew my new TV was smarter than I am because I couldn't even understand its remote control. It's black, and in the center is a little cube called the Smart Cube.

I'm not making this up.

All I'm doing is telling you what my TV tells me to.

If I press the Smart Cube, onto the screen pops something called the Smart Hub.

We get it.

My TV is smart, not humble.

I looked at the array of buttons on the Smart Hub, astounded. They were buttons I'd never seen before on a television, like Shop TV.

Wow.

It's not a television, it's a store.

I didn't push the Shop TV button, for obvious reasons. If I start buying things from my TV, my new address will be the poorhouse.

Which would not be Smart.

Then there's a button called Social TV, which I gather is for any parties my TV wants to attend or clubs it wants to join.

Like Mensa.

There is even a button for Fitness, which I fully intend to avoid, again for obvious reasons. I pressed it just to let you know what it says, and it contains something called Cardio Blast and Sexy Beach Abs.

Luckily I don't need either of these things.

My cardio is already blasted.

And I avoid sexy beaches.

Then there's a button called Schedule Manager, which sounded kind of controlling, but I checked it out. Immediately, a black box popped onto the screen which read, **Set the current time and date first**.

I found this tone so bossy, I opted out.

Not only that, I couldn't figure out how to do it.

If this TV is so damn smart, why doesn't it know the time and date?

I do.

So do you.

We rock!

There's even a button for a Web Browser, which I pushed and discovered that I could actually go on the computer from my television.

Incredible.

So my new TV is a store, a gym, a secretary, and a computer.

There's only one thing it isn't:

A book.

So it's not that smart, after all.

GOING, GOING, GONZO

BY LISA

I've always been addicted to garage sales and flea markets, but it turns out they were gateway drugs.

Now I'm hooked on auctions.

We begin a year ago, when I noticed there was an antiques auction in my neighborhood and I stopped by. I'm no antiques expert, but I like old things.

Like me.

So I walked into the auction, took a seat, and watched as the auctioneer showed slides of great furniture. Most of it was from the Philadelphia area, circa 1800s. People made bids by raising white cards, and when the bidding stopped, the prices weren't expensive at all.

Surprise ending, right?

I watched a beautiful mahogany end table from 1780 sell for $250.

What? Any piece of real solid mahogany from 1780 is worth $250, whether it's a table or a surf board.

Because it's a deal.

I watched equally amazed as a walnut tea table from 1760 went for $250.

Incredible!

I don't drink tea and I don't need a tea table, but so what? It was sad to see this great wood furniture go for such a low price, especially to someone not me.

That's what I started thinking, watching the auction. That the end tables deserved to be bought. That the chest of drawers needed a forever home.

I'd be rescuing this old authentic stuff, not merely buying it.

I'd be preserving the history of this great nation.

You can thank me anytime, United States.

So now I've discovered a whole new way of buying stuff I never wanted before I saw it for so cheap.

For example, take today. I went to the auction for a boot scrape, which is a metal thing that sits outside your front door and you use it to scrape mud off your shoes before you track it around your house. You may not think I need a boot scrape, but I will remind you that I live with five dogs, so I'm always stepping in something outside.

By the way, what I'm stepping in is never mud.

But "boot scrape" is a nicer term than "poop scrape."

So I got the boot scrape at the auction and was just about to leave when I couldn't believe the low prices that people were bidding for a mahogany writing table from 1830, which had an inclining slant top and four drawers with brass pulls.

If you don't know the pull of a brass pull, I can't explain it to you.

Plus it was called a writing desk, and I'm a writer.

I thought to myself, how can you buy a real mahogany writing desk for only $200?

Or more accurately, how could you not?

So I raised my hand.

And I'm now the proud owner of a mahogany writing desk. Never mind that I write with a laptop, so the desk's slant top is of no use.

I'm sure it will come in handy next time I use my quill.

Also the desk is colonial scale, so no normal chair will fit under it. Much less an ergonomic chair.

So it's not an economic desk.

But still, I put my printer on it, and it was a steal.

Of course, not everything at an auction is cheap, but you don't have to buy it, and going to an auction has entertainment value. For example, somebody at the auction bought a stuffed mountain goat for $1,200.

But I don't judge.

One man's trash is another man's treasure.

And I treasure all my trash.

HERE'S A HOWDY DO

BY FRANCESCA

I'm back on the dating scene and getting reacquainted with the art of presenting myself to new people.

The art of seduction begins with introduction.

Be open but don't ramble. Keep it light but keep it real. Be decisive, but let him lead.

Now if someone could just remind me what any of that means.

It shouldn't be this hard. I write about myself for a living, I ought to be able to tell a few winning stories about myself. But my only objective in writing to you, dear reader, is to make you laugh. I'm not trying to sleep with you.

Not necessarily.

I recently started seeing someone new, we've been on a handful of dates, and I like him so far. We had plans to go to dinner and a movie last Friday, but at 6:30 P.M.

that night, I still hadn't heard from him about which movie he picked, so I texted him.

"Sorry, I took a nap and just woke up," he replied. "Can we do Saturday instead?"

I had firm plans to stay in Saturday night, but I couldn't tell him why. The truth would reveal one of my dorkiest passions, not a fifth-date kind of revelation. Typically, I'll let you see me naked before I tell you this. But here goes:

I love Gilbert & Sullivan.

For those who got laid in high school, William S. Gilbert and Arthur Sullivan are the nineteenth-century writing team behind a series of comic operas. Their humor is satirical, heavy on wordplay, and aimed at lampooning Victorian England and mocking theatrical clichés of their day.

I know, I can't believe they fell out of favor either.

But take my word for it, Gilbert & Sullivan created some of the most beautiful classical music you will ever hear, and much of the humor is still relevant today.

Plus, the lyrics really improved my SAT Verbal score.

I was a member of the Gilbert & Sullivan Players in college, a group deemed nerdy even by Harvard standards, and I remain a fan.

Luckily, I don't have to be a dork alone. My closest guy friend is equally fanatic about G&S, so when he found a Facebook group called "Gilbert & Sullivan Sunday Singing Group," we both joined. This Sunday, they were singing through *The Mikado,* my favorite production. By overselling our talents via email, my friend had managed to get himself cast in the title role and me as the soprano lead, Yum-Yum.

Have I completely lost you? We're not allowed to sit at the same lunch table anymore, are we? It's okay, I understand, I'll eat this in the girls' bathroom.

So Saturday night I needed vocal rest and a good night's sleep before my performance. Although I was loath to admit it, I cared about this silly sing-along, a lot.

Singing Yum-Yum would serve some deep-seated psychological validation. When my high school did *Mikado,* I was cast as Yum-Yum's understudy. I practiced for hours, relishing every moment of rehearsals, fantasizing about performing the role. Of course, I never got to go on. This was my big chance to show the world I could do it.

Look who's singing in a living room in Brooklyn *now,* bitches!

I couldn't risk ruining my voice over drinks and conversation with a handsome dude.

This may be why I am single.

I felt lame twice over. First, because I got canceled on last minute, apparently losing out to the allure of a *nap,* and secondly, because I had such an uncool hobby. If this guy hadn't lost interest in me already, he sure would if I was honest with him, I thought.

So I lied, and vaguely said I had other plans.

I was true to myself, just not truthful to him.

Thankfully, by the time Sunday arrived, any boy trouble spinning in my brain was replaced by nervous excitement. My friend and I enjoyed a brunch of hot tea with honey and rode the subway together to Brooklyn, reassuring each other we were going to be great — just great! — as we fidgeted the whole way.

We arrived at an old brownstone near Prospect Park and walked up several creaking flights of stairs. When we arrived at the right floor, one door was ajar, and the sound of easy conversation wafted into the hallway.

Inside, the air was warm and humid, as ten or so people, most over the age of sixty, filled the small apartment. At first, my friend and I walked in all but unnoticed, but once we started introducing ourselves, everyone stopped to look at us. My friend asked about available scores, I went to get a glass of water, opening all the wrong cabinets until the hostess intervened, and we took our seats in the living room, shuffling our music on our laps.

Conversation had slowed to a trickle.

Then I understood. We were making them nervous.

Either with our youth or our foreignness, we had invaded their safe space. In our skinny jeans, we looked like the young, judgy idiots that most "cool" people under thirty usually are.

Little did they know.

"So," I said, hoping to break the ice, "how did we all get into G&S?"

I shared that I've been listening to the music since I was in the womb, thanks to my mother, and recounted that when my high school announced our spring musical was *The Mikado,* I was the only fifteen-year-old to fist-pump and cry, "YES!"

That a got a laugh.

"Are you a student in college now?" asked one man.

"No, I'm twenty-eight," I said with a

wince. "But thanks!"

He shrugged, as if it made no difference.

My friend told about how we met in college, when we were both in the chorus of *Pirates of Penzance,* and how he almost dropped me on my head during the choreography.

"I survived," I said, "and we've been friends ever since."

Having established our credentials, the rest of the room opened up. One man talked about learning the music in elementary school.

"They used to teach this music in schools, in our day," he said.

"My son played the Major General in *Pirates* when he was at sleepaway camp," said one woman.

"Does he still like singing in shows?" I asked.

"He doesn't perform anymore. He's forty now and lives in New Jersey."

Another woman shared a picture of herself in costume for Yum-Yum with members from this very group, and, judging from their hairstyles, it looked like it was taken in the seventies. She said, "This was before my second marriage, do you remember that, Frances?"

I began to understand that these people

had been meeting up for Gilbert & Sullivan committee meetings, sing-alongs, and all the friendship in between, for well over thirty years. They'd seen each other through marriages, and second marriages, and children growing old.

And they had done it singing.

I couldn't think of anything cooler.

Everyone had an assigned role, and we sang through the entire opera, including the dialogue scenes, with a short intermission to snack on watermelon, cheese, and — not for the faint of heart — smoked oysters.

None of us were professional singers, but what we lacked in talent, we made up for in enthusiasm. The spirit of the room was encouraging and supportive. I blushed the time when I didn't quite make a high note, but everyone clapped at the end anyway. And I was impressed at how these once-shy adults sang out at full volume. Normally I'm so shy about my neighbors hearing me, I don't sing at full volume in my own shower. The Gilbert & Sullivan Sunday Singers left the door open.

By the time my friend and I said our goodbyes and promises to return, my voice was hoarse.

On the train ride home, I saw that the guy who canceled had texted me to make plans the following week — maybe he did like me after all. Still, I'm not sure I'll follow up. I might be too cool for him.

In Search of Selfie
BY LISA

Everyone is buzzing with the news that there are hundreds of leaked celebrity nude selfies being posted on the Internet.

Celebrities are leaking, people.

You may have read about it. There's a lot of really pretty models and actresses who are now appearing in various states of undress on the Internet, for all to see. It goes without saying that this is a terrible invasion of their privacy, and they want to retain the right to invade their own privacy.

Which I get.

I looked at these photos, to see what all the fuss is about, and the pictures show these women taking selfies in their camisoles and nothing else, or in their bras and nothing else, or in their underwear and nothing else, and at one point or another, they're all sucking on their finger.

I have several thoughts.

First, when will the sucking-on-the-finger

thing get old?

WHEN?

Ladies, don't do it anymore.

Don't.

The same goes for sucking on bananas, Popsicles, and straws.

Really, do we not get this yet?

WE GET IT.

It's hard to claim to be a feminist if you're sucking your finger.

Because you can't talk.

Second, I'm trying to understand what the celebrities were thinking when they took these pictures. All I ever read about is celebrities whining that photographers are taking too many pictures of them, or that people on the street are taking too many pictures of them, or that everything is about pictures of them, yet as soon as these celebrities get near an underwire bra or some fresh laundry, they're snapping even more pictures of themselves.

MAKE UP YOUR MINDS, CELEBRITIES.

Evidently there are never enough pictures for celebrities, or for all of the other knuckleheads who are taking nude selfies all the time.

Does no one have hobbies anymore?

Does no one go for walks?

How about a bike ride?

Or to the library, or the mall?

Why is taking a nude selfie such a compelling activity?

DON'T YOU KNOW WHAT YOU LOOK LIKE NAKED?

TAKE OFF YOUR CLOTHES AND LOOK DOWN.

And, if you don't want naked pictures of yourself to exist:

DON'T TAKE NAKED PICTURES OF YOURSELF.

I'm not blaming the victim, I'm being a good mom to the victim.

In a perfect world, nude selfies would be a great idea. But we live in a world that contains Mace, self-defense classes, and the NSA.

PROTECT YOURSELF.

FROM YOURSELF.

AND EVERYBODY ELSE.

And if the celebrity sends the naked selfie she has taken to her boyfriend, is it really that different from every other naked picture she's posed for in magazines, newspapers, blogs, or in about 3 million other places?

For example, one of the people whose naked selfies were leaked is Kate Upton, a model who has posed topless lots of places, including *Sports Illustrated.*

The sports are illustrated, the women are naked.

Maybe the complaint is that she didn't get paid for the nude selfie, as opposed to the nude photo, which I get.

Because another thing that never gets old is money.

IT NEVER GETS OLD.

Another actress said she took a nude selfie of herself for her boyfriend. But here's what I have to say to her boyfriend:

DO YOU REALLY NEED A PHOTO TO REMEMBER WHAT YOUR GIRL-FRIEND LOOKS LIKE?

I mean, how bad is your memory, dude?

Not to mention your imagination?

The celebrity selfies were hacked from the cloud, which is another thing it's impossible to understand. That movie trailer was right, nobody understands the cloud, least of all me, and I pay for a yearly cloud subscription.

Yes, I'm a cloud subscriber.

The cloud is supposed to back up my phone, laptop, and desktop computer every time I sync it, but that never works.

Maybe because I don't have any nude selfies of me sucking my finger.

Also sync is now a word.

This is not progress.

188

Anyway, to stay on point, what I have are 3 zillion pictures of my dogs and cats doing adorable things, and my bet is that the cloud is full to bursting with such things, so that when it starts raining, yes, you guessed it, it will rain cats and dogs.

And nude selfies.

Also, fingers, bananas, and a Popsicle.

And all I have to say is:

STEP AWAY FROM THE SELFIE.

AND READ.

This Is Your Dog on Drugs

BY LISA

I am the old woman who lived in a shoe, who had so many dogs she didn't know what to do.

Okay, not exactly, but I'm having dog issues.

In that the dogs are all wonderful individually, but together, it's a zoo.

And I know it's politically incorrect, but I think it might be gender-related.

Let me give you some context.

A few years ago I had three wonderful golden retrievers, all of whom were female. They were always happy and they never fought with each other. Goldens think that life is a party and they're the guest of honor, and you're always welcome if you bring a keg.

Sadly, the goldens passed away, and I found myself in collect-them-all mode with four Cavalier King Charles Spaniels, which are adorable little dogs, but somehow I ended up with three boys — Tony, Boone, and Kit — and one female, Peach.

Ruby The Corgi is a female too, but her issues are unrelated to gender.

There's a reason corgis are Queen Elizabeth's favorite dog.

And I bet they push her royal ass around.

Anyway, it turns out that testosterone can be toxic.

The three boys fight, and the most aggressive is Boone. He was previously my adorably goofy puppy, but he's growing into his full alpha-male self and has become a tiny terror. About a month ago he started picking on his smaller brother, Kit, attacking him for no reason at all. I consulted my girlfriends, plus a dog trainer and my vet, all of whom told me I had to deal with the situation before it got out of control.

So I put a harness and a leash on Boone at all times, even inside the house, where we were tied together all day. If I ate lunch, there was a leash on my wrist. Same with dinner. I had him with me even when I went to the bathroom.

To be fair, this last part isn't a change.

No dog owner has privacy in the bathroom.

I used to read on the toilet, but now I pet.

The worst incident took place a month

ago, when Boone lunged after Kit with me on the other end of the leash. It yanked me off balance because I'm a klutz, and before I knew it, Boone and Kit were fighting, Tony and Peach had joined the fray, and Ruby ordered everybody to debtors' prison.

I rolled around on the kitchen floor with five dogs, all of whom were fighting, like a big rolling ball of bad news.

The Cavaliers have tiny teeth, but I still had to take Tony to the emergency vet for a bite on his ear.

He was fine, I'd had it. Besides which, I work at home, and you can imagine that not a lot of words get written when you type with a growling dog attached to your wrist.

They say that we make our own prison, but I hadn't felt that way since Thing One and Thing Two.

And you can't divorce your dogs.

Nor do you really want to.

So I went back to the vet, and he had a great idea.

Medication.

I told him I was already on Crestor but I was open to suggestions.

It turns out he was talking about the dog.

The vet said Boone's problems were due to anxiety, and I guess I didn't appreciate how stressful it was to choose whether you want to eat, sleep, or chew underwear.

So now Boone is on Prozac. I give him a pill every day with peanut butter, but he has to sit.

I train my dog with antidepressants.

You may remember a while ago that Ruby was on Prozac, which didn't work. This time, I'm happy to report that Prozac worked for Boone.

Better dogs through chemistry.

Boone is back to his old, goofy, lovable, non-aggressive self.

A *very* happy ending.

WORKING OUT
ON MOUNT OLYMPUS
BY FRANCESCA

This summer, I've gone to the gym six days a week, sometimes seven. What's my secret to staying motivated?

Hot fitness instructors.

I'm seeing several. I'm monogamous in romance but promiscuous with group fitness classes.

I've yet to meet an ugly trainer. Phenomenal physical shape is a given, and in New York, most are also actors, dancers, and other professionally attractive jobs.

Thank goodness I'm a writer.

My first fitness love was Edu. He was head-to-toe gorgeous, with muscles like a superhero.

I had to let him measure my body-fat percentage with pincers on my belly, which took superhuman humility.

I wish we could've worked out with the lights off.

Stunning fitness professionals come in

every flavor, and I'm determined to taste them all.

Gregg is my sexy drill sergeant: buzz cut, square jaw, V-torso, not a bad angle on him. He teaches a class called "Whipped" that I only wish was literal.

Philippe is the spin instructor that makes me dizzy. He's a green-eyed pretty boy, perfectly buff, tan, and hairless, like he was born Photoshopped.

There are always several women loitering after class to ask Philippe a pretend question. It's pathetic.

Especially when someone steals my pretend question.

I'm equally enamored with the women. Story teaches a strength class and looks like Barbie with better delts.

But Aida is my main fitness crush object. A bohemian gypsy in leg warmers, she teaches Pilates with a Spanish accent. Imagine strengthening your core with Penelope Cruz.

For the first month of class, I thought she was telling us to "excel," which I found encouraging. Then I understood we were to "exhale."

For Aida, I can only sigh.

Have you noticed their unusual names? These are names befitting the gods and goddesses that they are.

My gym is Mount Olympus, with a monthly fee.

We are but their mortal playthings. They control our heart rate, how's that for playing God?

I'm happy to do their bidding. A simple, "That's eet!" from Aida can make my day. I want to impress her so badly, I bought a book, *Anatomy of Pilates,* to cram for class.

I'm such a nerd, I can't even be a jock without studying.

I feel an instant sense of camaraderie with the other class members, and I'm fiercely loyal to my favorite instructors.

I think I could be very susceptible to a cult.

My loyalty was tested last week, when a girl disrupted our Pilates class by packing up early. Aida asked if she could wait, "Please, eet ees only five minutes."

The girl muttered, loud enough for everyone to hear, "Bitch."

I gasped, expecting lightning to strike.

"Excuse me, what ees your name?" Aida's voice was as sweet as *crema Catalana,* but everyone knew she could break this chick in half.

The girl wisely fled. She'd better hope she never runs into me in the locker room.

Yet, all great love stories end in sorrow. I learned yesterday that Aida is leaving me. She's moving to L.A.

My heartbreak is as operatic as her name. Verdi had it right: I want to lock us in a pyramid and do mat Pilates with her until death do us part.

But I'm grateful. Saint Aida performed two miracles in my life. First, she made me like my stomach, a body part I've hated since 1999. Second, she made me feel powerful after a period when I'd felt my most helpless.

The dual experience of breaking up with a man I loved and caring for my adored grandmother while knowing that she wouldn't get better felt like an exercise in failure. By the time I returned to New York after her passing, I was fifteen pounds heavier on the scale and about a hundred pounds heavier in my heart. In helping me rebuild my body, these instructors reminded me that I'm capable of improvement, adaptation, and strength.

Aida taught me that even when you're flat on your back, you can pull yourself up. One vertebra at a time.

An App a Day

BY LISA

These days, all you need to lose weight is diet, exercise, and a smartphone.

You know what I'm talking about?

Haven't you noticed the trend?

I haven't, either.

Daughter Francesca keeps me abreast of such things, so that I can sound remotely relevant at cocktail parties, which I never attend and doubt even exist anymore.

We begin when I was on my last diet, and Francesca told me that the best way to lose weight was to use an app that was free for your phone, called Lose It!

Unfortunately, I lost it.

Not the app, but the phone.

By the way, the exclamation mark is part of the Lose It! name. Don't think I'm all excited about a diet!

Because I'm not!

I'm excited about food!

Not diets!

And most of the time, I don't Lose It! but Gain It!

Anyway, the way the Lose It! app works is simple.

First, you have to tell it your weight.

Second, you're not allowed to lie.

Right there is the problem.

I never tell anybody my real weight, not even an inanimate object, but you can tell the app that you're five pounds less than what you really are, so in case somebody finds your phone, you have wiggle room.

Just not in your jeans.

And after you tell the app your weight, then it asks you how much weight you want to lose, and when you tell it your goal weight, it laughs for the next fifteen minutes.

Just kidding.

But then, through some complex mathematical process, the app figures out how many calories you're allowed per day, in order to reach your goal weight by the end of the century.

Lose It! gave me one thousand five hundred calories a day, which I rapidly discovered gets me through midmorning.

Because every day you have to record what you ate, and this being America, it tells you exactly what calories, carbs, grams of sugar, protein, saturated fats, red dye, and rodent hair you have consumed each day.

If you're me, you will faithfully record what you ate for two days, then you'll start forgetting to record anything.

Which means you ate nothing.

Just like when something doesn't have a price tag on it, it's free.

On the plus side, you're also supposed to record any exercise you did, and the app automatically knows how many calories are consumed by the exercise you chose, so it deducts it from the mountain of food that you ate.

I say this is good news, because I found that whenever I did any exercise at all, I was very happy to record it in the app. But since I wasn't recording any of the food I ate, many of my days showed a negative calorie count, and I reached my goal weight in minus three days.

That is, at least according to the app.

So I gave up.

Obviously, the way these things work is that you're supposed to be accountable for what you eat, and I sure hope this craze passes quickly.

Except that the other day, Daughter Francesca told me that there's a new weight-loss app and it's called My Fitness Pal.

She told me to give it a whirl, so I went

on, got the app, and determined that it works basically the same way as Lose It!, except it has one horrible innovation that I didn't know about until I got an email from Francesca that read:

MOM, AREN'T YOU GOING TO RECORD YOUR CALORIES TODAY?

I called her instantly, surprised. "How do you know I didn't record any calories?"

Francesca chuckled. "Because with this application, I can see the diet and exercise you record every day. But you're not recording anything."

"What?" I asked, horrified. "You're *inside* my app?"

"Yes, when you signed on, you gave me access."

Big mistake, I thought, but didn't say.

"Mom, I gave you access and you can look inside my app, too. Whenever you want to, you can see what I'm eating."

I stopped doing that when you were three years old, was another thing I thought but didn't say.

Because my daughter is My Fitness Pal.

And there are now special bracelets, activity trackers, and a zillion new apps and gadgets that will keep track of our calories, exercise, and dirty thoughts.

I'm keeping mine to my chubby little self.

I'm Spending My Granddog's Inheritance

BY LISA

I'm babysitting my granddog.

Yes, you read that right.

I don't have any grandchildren, but I have a granddog, a little boy aged five, and he looks just like me.

Our noses are identical. They're large and they leak.

My granddog's name is Pip, and you may know he's Daughter Francesca's furry son, but he gets all his best traits from me.

Namely, begging at the table.

You haven't lived until you've eaten dinner with me, because the whole time, my eyes are on your plate.

This could be the reason for my lack of dating success.

God knows why, but men don't get turned on when I lean over and whisper in their ear, "Aren't you going to eat that?"

The other trait I share with my granddog is that we do the same tricks, in that we both

Sit and Lie Down.

But we don't Fetch unless there's a sale.

And we don't Roll Over for anybody.

I know that people love having grandchildren, and some of my friends say that having grandchildren is even better than having children. Plus, one out of every three bumper stickers is about grandchildren.

Or honor students.

Or honor-student grandchildren.

And the other day, one of my readers happened to say to me, "When is Francesca going to give you grandchildren?"

I was at a loss for words.

At least temporarily.

I never thought of grandchildren as something that Francesca would give me, and all of a sudden, I realized what I was missing.

I was missing an opportunity to guilt-trip my daughter about something, which shows what kind of mother I am.

Only a bad mother misses a chance to guilt-trip her kid.

But I have to say, although I'm sure I'll love being a grandparent, I'm not there yet.

Not that I'm not a huge fan of babies, because I am.

I coo at every baby I see in the supermarket in the shopping cart, on the sidewalk in strollers, and even on the bike trail, where they get towed along in little carriers.

Babies are always on the move.

But I'm not ready for grandchildren yet, and not for the conventional reason. I don't mind getting older, and I want my future grandchild to call me grandma.

Either that, or Mrs. Bradley Cooper.

But at the same time, I'm divorced twice, and I know that it's important to choose the right mate the first time.

And the second time, too.

I'm looking forward to choosing the right mate the third time, because after three strikes, I get three more at bats, isn't that how it works?

So I'm not guilt-tripping Daughter Francesca over not giving me grandchildren because even after my divorces, I still believe in marriage. And what I've learned from Thing One and Thing Two, or at least being married and divorced from them, is that I should have taken my time.

I should've taken my time when I was dating, and I should've taken my time when I said I do.

In those days, I never did anything on my time. I did it on everybody else's time, and I don't think I'm the only woman who made that mistake in her younger days.

Please tell me you know what I'm talking about.

But the wisdom of being a grandparent's age, even if you're not a grandparent yet, is that you don't have to do anything on command.

Nobody can rush you into anything, whether it's getting engaged or getting married, or whether you want to see those shoes in your size.

I believe that older people know this, and you can test my theory yourself, simply by getting in line behind a senior citizen.

They're in no hurry.

They're not going to rush.

They're taking their time.

And you know what?

They're not dull or slow.

On the contrary, they're smarter than all of us.

So I'm taking a lesson from older people everywhere, as well as from dogs, and I sense that Francesca is, too.

So I'm not rushing her.

I'm not even rushing my granddog.

For now, we'll all Stay.

THE REBOUND

BY FRANCESCA

Getting your hair pulled out by a lunatic isn't what most people would consider a good omen. But lately I'm not one easily kept down.

I guess you could say I'm on the rebound.

My friend invited me to a rooftop party expressly for singles, what in high school we called a "mixer." Fresh from my breakup, it was out of my comfort zone but seemed like something I should say yes to.

I decided to flip my thinking and declare it my Single Gal Deb Ball, the event where I'd re-present myself to New York as an eligible lady.

I even wore a white dress.

The dress stopped six inches north of my knees, but, c'mon. We're not in Kansas anymore.

My two girlfriends and I decided to meet for a glass of wine to gird ourselves for the night ahead. It was an unusually warm night, and we staked out a table beside the open window, with me sitting closest to the street. My Sauvignon Blanc had barely broken a sweat when it happened. I never saw it coming.

A man on the street ran by, reached through the window, grabbed a fistful of my hair, and yanked it full force, almost clear out of my head.

At first, all I felt was being pulled backwards, hard. My first reaction was to slam my hand down on my purse.

Because I'm a real New Yorker.

And as soon as I realized the pain was coming from my scalp, my next thought was, "Did he mess up my hair?"

Because I'm a real girl.

Although the dude pulled my hair hard enough to induce whiplash worse than being rear-ended in a car, my hair hadn't come out.

Next Pantene spokeswoman, right here.

When I realized I wasn't being mugged, the attack was over, and I was not bleeding from the head, I finally registered the pain. "OW!"

My friends sat across me, their mouths in identical o's of horror.

"Ohmigod, are you okay?"

"You were just legit assaulted!"

207

Whoever said the Lower East Side lost its grit when the Whole Foods arrived has never had a drive-by tweaker try and rip their hair out.

Let it be noted that the couple at the table right next to us stared at me but said nothing. The man was sitting right beside me when it happened, and he didn't even ask me if I was okay.

I hoped his girlfriend was paying attention.

"Should you call the police?" asked my friend.

I tried to shake my head, but it hurt. "Nah." The truth was, I didn't get a good look at the guy, he'd disappeared into the crowded streets seconds after it happened and was long gone by now. "The cops would probably ask me what my hair was wearing."

"Your hair *was* kind of asking for it." My friend giggled.

I realized I could either let this freak occurrence ruin my night, or I could do what I came to do — rebound.

I was a soldier of fun.

Before I could change my mind, I gulped the rest of my wine — nature's Advil — and we headed to the mixer.

The mixer was held in an incredibly dark,

loud bar — perfect for getting to know new people!

Not that I had a chance to survey our options anyway. I'd tweeted a joke about my hair-puller on the way over, and inadvertently prompted a flurry of anxious text messages from my mom. As I tapped away on my phone, trying to reassure her so we didn't graduate to panicked calls, I hoped I looked busy and in demand.

That's why we have phones, right?

We noticed some photographers taking pictures of three really, really tall men, the international sign for basketball players. The three of us looked at each other with the identical thought — why not?

I'm wary of professional athletes as boyfriend prospects. I think they have it too easy. But one thing basketball players are good at?

That's right — the rebound.

So I let myself be chatted up, or, since he was six-foot-seven, chatted down by Darren, an American who plays professionally in Ireland. Being the best basketball player in Ireland might be like being the best surfer in Switzerland, but I was still impressed. And he was actually very nice and down-to-earth. At one point, he asked how old I was.

"I'm twenty-eight," I said.

"Wow. You look twenty-six."

This made me laugh — such precision! — but Darren looked at me quizzically. But I guess pro athletes meet enough women to easily size up our player stats. He probably knew my height, weight, and cup size too.

It was time to bounce.

But not before he got my number.

We moved on to a different bar, where a group of my girlfriend's childhood pals were hanging out. "They have dancing," my friend said.

I didn't know if I was up for dancing in the sky-high, mint green, strappy heels I was wearing.

Then I had a beer — nature's dance instructor.

So I broke it down on the dance floor, but mostly by myself. No one would dance with me. Even the friends I came with had formed a circle that I ended up outside of.

The men at this new bar were apparently immune to my twenty-eight-looks-twenty-six mojo.

Maybe everyone was twenty-five and a half.

But tonight was the night of flipping my thinking. So instead of viewing myself as radioactive, I decided I was a free radical.

Either my attitude adjustment improved

my dance moves or I looked like a weakened gazelle, but I caught a guy looking at me from across the room. He was tall, thin, and blond, and his long, angular limbs gave his dancing a comical bent. I thought he looked like Gumby, but not unattractive. He was Hot Gumby.

When I met his gaze, Hot Gumby did the double-fisted point at me. In a generous mood, I pointed back and mimicked his silly dance moves, which I became increasingly unsure were silly on purpose. He shimmied over to me like one of those blow-up tube-men at a car dealership.

He introduced himself, but the music was so loud, I had no clue what he said, even after making him repeat it twice.

Hot Gumby, it is.

"Where do you think I'm from?" he asked, grinning.

I had no clue, and I told him so.

"Guess!"

Outer space? "I really have no idea."

"GERMANY!" he cried.

Okay, German Gumby.

This guy was not my soul mate, but he was sweet, in a foreign-exchange-student way, so I gave him my number.

(We've since been platonic text-message pen pals. I'm helping him with his English, and he tells me what's happening in soccer whether I care or not.)

But that night, talking with Gumby had broken the seal, and suddenly a lot of dudes wanted to dance with me — all creeps.

Men are like magnets, you need one to repel one.

I tapped one of the guys in our circle of friends who I had met a few times and liked. I thought he looked like a ginger Matt Damon.

"Will you dance with me for a minute?" I asked.

"Me? Really?"

I mean, how charming is that?

Dancing with him, I had more fun than I had had all night. Making the first move is awesome — no wonder men do it.

We danced until my feet hurt, and I'd forgotten all about the missing patch of hair at the back of my head.

You can't control if a guy lets you down, or if the boy likes you back, or even if a psycho pulls your hair.

You can only control the rebound.

I'm gonna play.

BIRTHDAY PRESENT

BY LISA

It was my birthday this week, and I celebrated by almost getting arrested.

Our story begins at three o'clock in the afternoon, on a day that was blazing hot — eighty-seven degrees to be precise. I pulled into a parking lot and noticed that the black car next to me had an adorable little white dog inside. But the car windows were only cracked an inch and the dog looked frantic, jumping around and panting profusely. The car seats were dotted with saliva. You didn't have to be a vet to know that the dog was in obvious distress.

I didn't see the dog's owner anywhere. I hurried into the store, looked around, and told the shopkeeper. They made an announcement, but the dog's owner wasn't in the store. I went back to the car and stuck my hand in the cracked window, and it barely fit. I could feel how ungodly hot it was in the car. The dog pawed the window, frantically.

So you know me, I called 911. Amazingly, the police arrived in about ten minutes, and by then I was frantic, too. "Officer," I told him, "can you please get one of those tools you guys use, to open the window and unlock the door?"

"No, I'm sorry, I can't. Our procedure is to find the owner."

"But I tried and this dog could die."

I was already taking off my clog and trying to figure out if it could smash a car window.

"Let me try to find the owner," the cop said.

So I ran back inside the store, to look for a blunt object, but when I came back outside, the dog's owner had returned, a thirtysomething man who sauntered slowly toward his car, his pasty face expressionless. This, even though his dog was in obvious distress, a police officer and his cruiser were on the scene, and a small crowd had gathered.

By the way, the man was sipping bottled water.

His dog had no water bottle.

So you can imagine how this went down.

I didn't get arrested, though I tried.

The cop said to the man, "Sir, it's very

hot to leave a dog in a car."

The man answered coolly, "I was only gone half an hour. I was at the gym."

I yelled at the man, "A *half hour* is too long for a dog to be in a car in this heat! A dog can die in a car in only *five minutes*! Are you a *complete idiot*? What is the *matter* with you? Don't you watch the news? Open the door! This is *animal cruelty*!"

I also added a lot of really good profanity, and even so, it wasn't as much as the man deserved.

The cop asked me not to make a scene.

I told the cop he hadn't seen anything yet.

The cop asked me to back away.

I told the cop I wasn't going anywhere.

Then the cop backed me away, gently.

Gulp.

Okay, so I stayed backed away, but I kept yelling at the man. From a distance, which was even better.

The cop asked the man his name and address, and even as the man gave the cop his information, he refused to open the door for the overheated dog.

I kept yelling at the man and I told the cop I wanted to file a complaint of animal cruelty.

The cop told me that wouldn't be possible, and since I was already yelling at the man, I didn't start yelling at the cop too, because that would ruin my credibility. Also, the cop was just doing his job, unlike the psychopath who had left his dog to suffer in a car.

In the end, the psychopath drove away, and his poor little dog went with him. And I can only hope that one night, when he's asleep, the dog bites him.

And if the dog doesn't, I will.

Because it's taken me fifty-nine years to learn that sometimes, you have to stand up.

And yell.

Happy birthday to me.

Rescue Me

BY LISA

I just wrote about a villain.

Now, I'm writing about a hero.

And an incredibly good-looking one, which figures into the story, as you will see.

We begin on Sunday morning, when I meet my bestie Franca for a bike ride. We've been friends through thirty years, and between us we have four divorces, which is a nice even number.

We love to do things together and are very much alike, except that Franca is an incredible athlete and runs five miles every day.

That would be the end of the similarity.

There is nothing I do every day that lasts five miles, if you don't count running back and forth to the refrigerator.

Nevertheless, Franca and I have become bicycling buddies, which means that we meet at a parking lot, lather up with sunscreen, hop on our bikes, and ride side by side on the trail, yapping the whole time.

I consider this exercise, and as you can imagine, my tongue is in incredible shape.

Anyway, this particular trail is paved the whole route, and it leaves from the Wegman's, which makes it the perfect trail, because after the ride we get to have lunch, food shop, or have lunch while we food shop, which we have actually done.

In any event, Franca and I were riding our bicycles along the trail, and we were almost six miles out when I got a flat tire. Actually, it took me a few minutes to notice because I was working out my tongue.

This presented a real problem, because neither of us knew what to do next, and we would have to walk all the way back to Wegman's, which would take about eighty-five hours and be no fun at all.

We had barely pulled over to the side of the trail and started whining to each other when a man who was riding his bike in the opposite direction stopped and asked us if we wanted help.

This is where you find out that even though I'm a feminist, I'm a bad feminist.

Because I not only wanted help, I wanted to be rescued.

I wanted somebody to make it all better, so I didn't have to figure it out myself, even if I could.

I wanted a white knight, and for once in my life, there he was. He even had a white helmet on and his bicycle was white, too. Also his shirt, and his coat of armor.

So I answered, "Yes, please help us, kind sir and liege lord." Or words to that effect.

He got off his bike, leaned it against a tree, and strode over, and as he got closer, I knew I couldn't look at Franca or I would burst out laughing because we were both thinking the same thing — that this was easily the best-looking man on the planet.

Okay, it least, it was the best-looking man I've seen in a long time, if you don't count Bradley Cooper.

And I can't tell you the last time Bradley Cooper fixed my flat.

No joke, this guy had gorgeous blue eyes, beautifully chiseled cheekbones, and a confident, dazzling smile. Not only that, he was six-foot-five inches of pure muscle, his biceps rippling under a tight cycling jersey that was unzipped to reveal the perfect amount of chest hair.

I know that we ladies have varying opinions about chest hair, and I don't impose my view on you. You just fill in the blank about what is the perfect amount for you because I'm telling you right now, no matter what you think about chest hair, this man would've changed your mind.

As for the rest of his body, I am not going to tell you what he looked like in spandex bicycle shorts, because you're not old enough.

Just use your imagination.

All I can say is he is the reason God made spandex.

And when he came over and took my flabby tire in his strong and manly hand, I spotted his wedding ring and blurted out, "Of course you're married."

"What?" He looked up, slightly puzzled.

Franca burst into laughter. "She's just kidding. She likes to joke around."

"Not all the time," I tell her, and we both laughed like idiots.

I'm not sure what happened next, and Franca couldn't tell you either, because we were both woozy from the fumes off his testosterone, but he changed the bike tire in three minutes, explaining to us what he was doing, as if we could concentrate on anything he was saying.

And he even gave me an innertube, which I will treasure forever.

Or at least until I get my next flat tire, as soon as possible.

Rite of Train Passage

BY FRANCESCA

My friend invited me to her rental house in the Hamptons for the Fourth of July.

Fireworks went off in my heart.

I've been dying to go to the Hamptons ever since I moved to New York five years ago, and I'm so proud that my friends have now reached a level in their careers where I can mooch off them.

But in order to experience this quintessential New Yorker getaway, one must endure the rite of passage that is getting there.

I left Thursday night via the Montauk line of the Long Island Railroad, or the LIRR. I felt young and fabulous leaving for my classy holiday. I carried a floppy straw hat as unofficial passport.

But the aura of glamour disappeared once I boarded, because I was sharing a train car with some of the most dangerous thugs on earth:

Teenage girls.

Two of them. A pack.

These two girls were talking very loudly, which sounds like a real Grandma complaint, but I'm telling you, they were projecting for the stage — and Shakespeare it was *not.* I believe they were performing the play, *Talking Sh*t About Everyone.*

Based on the swearing, I think it's an early work of Harold Pinter.

While I struggled to read my book, I dug deep to summon goodwill toward these girls. They're young, they're having fun, I'm sure I was like that once.

"What I don't get is like, people who say big is beautiful. Like, fat is not healthy. And you look ugly."

Never mind. I would've hated these girls when I was their age, too.

When one let out an earsplitting squeal, I glanced back and locked eyes with a curly-haired woman unfortunate enough to be sitting behind them.

The woman made a face like, *Can you believe them?*

I returned the sentiment with eyes like, *I know, right?*

But then something awful happened. The curly-haired woman gave me a nod, and before I could stop her, she scolded the girls

222

with a loud, librarian-ish, *Shhhh.*

The Heathers were silent for a beat before redirecting their laser-snark at the poor woman. They mean-girled her for the rest of the ride.

"Wait," my friend interrupted as I told him the story. "Did you step in to defend her?"

"I didn't tell her to do it!" I cried.

"But it was your validation that inspired the shush. She thought you had her back."

"I was two rows away! I was out of the zone of responsibility!"

But he was right. Knowing I had many more stops to go, I was a coward. I had spent enough time hiding in the bathroom in sixth grade.

Mercifully, the woman's stop came soon after, and she was free to leave and call her therapist.

Meanwhile, the girls expanded their abuse to the entire train car.

"BRR!" one girl yelled, turning shivering into an interpretive dance. "THIS TRAIN IS TOO COLD FOR US SKINNIES! ALL THESE FATTIES DON'T UNDER-STAND!"

Charming, no?

And from their endless "Are we there yet?" whining, I ascertained their stop was the very last on the line.

We can only hope they were going to the moon.

So instead of feeling young and fabulous, I spent the rest of the ride feeling both frightened and old.

Once I made it to Sag Harbor, I had a wonderful July Fourth weekend with my friends. We barbecued every food group, pretended to be soccer fans, played stupid drinking games — everything our forefathers would have wanted. But come Sunday, I had to again brave public transit back to the city.

I knew the LIRR would be crowded the Sunday after July Fourth, but this was Xtreme Train Riding. It was as if the entire population of Manhattan had squeezed into eight train cars.

Every seat was taken and the aisles were packed with people, standing room only. Even the short staircase between the upper and lower levels was stacked with squatters. One woman crouched on the stairs shot daggers to anyone who dared try to go up or down, as if *they* were being unreasonable.

This train would make a sardine can look like the Ritz-Carlton.

I snagged a spot to stand near the doors.

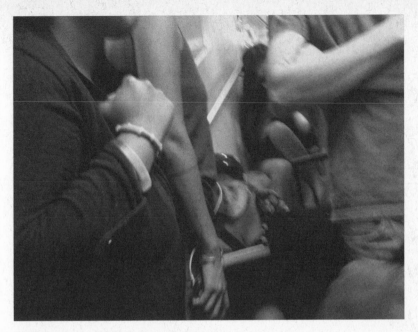

I bought a ticket for this?

For the first hour and a half, there wasn't enough room for me to fit both legs on one side of my suitcase, so I was forced to straddle it.

The Hamptons didn't seem so classy anymore.

Clown cars have more leg room.

I'd say there wasn't a spare inch, but when a visibly drunk young man with a hat reading #YOLO squeezed his way to the end of our car and slurred, "Where's the bathroom?" our collective recoil revealed a bit more space.

So there was no question the train car was

at capacity, but when we hit South Hampton, a mother and her teenage daughter decided they were going to fit on. Believe and you shall achieve, kids, because, somehow they did it. As I was the closest to the door, that meant we stood nearly nose to nose.

I've never been so close to someone I wasn't about to make out with. If the lighting had been better, we just might have.

And this is when I realized the LIRR is the great equalizer of the Hamptons' varied inhabitants. The mother was dripping in diamonds. Diamond-stud earrings so large they pulled at her earlobes. A chain of linked diamonds draped over her tunic as casually as a lanyard. Stacked diamond rings on her fingers, each as big as a signet ring.

Having just helped my best friend's boyfriend choose an engagement ring, I am now a certified amateur gemologist, and by my estimation, her diamond earrings were about a gazillion carats.

I confess I was so curious about these people that when I spotted their name on their luggage tag, I Googled them on my iPhone.

Yes, standing right next to them.

Rude, I know, and risky, but if the mom turned out to be a publishing tycoon, I might try and make out with her after all.

She wasn't.

But they turned out to be very nice. As we were practically chest bumping the entire drive, we struck up a friendly rapport. We commiserated about the slow train, our travel connections, I had an Amtrak to Philly to catch, they had a plane to Paris to board.

I have a hunch it was private.

But for the next two hours, we were all equal in the eyes of the Long Island Railroad. One train car, under God, indivisible, with liberty and justice for all.

RECYCLED

BY LISA

More misadventures on a bicycle, from your favorite rookie cyclist.

If you recall, I went bicycle riding with my best friend Franca about a week ago, and I got a lucky flat tire that gave me the opportunity to meet the handsomest man on earth, my Knight on the White Bicycle.

He fixed my tire, and by that I mean he fixed my tire.

Nothing else happened.

Recall that he is married and I am the most middle-aged woman on earth.

Nobody is breaking his vows for my cellulite.

Frankly, that's fine with me. There are lines I won't cross, and that's one of them.

Another one is the third piece of chocolate cake. If I'm on my fourth, I know I'm in trouble.

Also my fifth.

Okay, maybe I'd cross the chocolate-cake

line, but I never cheat on my taxes.

Really.

The IRS lacks a sense of humor.

Also, jail time.

Anyway, to return to the story, Franca and I were cycling when we approached the spot where the trail ends at a sharp curve, a traffic light, and the intersection of Route 202, Route 252, and certain death.

This intersection always makes me nervous, and the last time we came to this traffic light, Franca fell off her bike and skinned her knee. So as we approached, I called out to her, "Careful, honey!"

She turned around to ask, "What did you say?"

And in that moment, she crossed into the intersection, crashed her bike, and fell exactly where she had fallen before, skinning the same knee. Not only that but I crashed into her, falling over, and skinning my elbow where I had skinned it before, too.

If you think it's easy to injure yourself in the exact same place twice in a row, you're wrong.

It's a skill that few people possess, namely only Franca and me.

In any event, Franca and I were lying in a crumpled mess in the intersection, our limbs bloodied and our bicycles bent up. Traffic stopped, only because Franca is so hot.

I'm not just saying this because she's my best friend.

She is superhot, and anybody who bicycles will tell you that traffic will not stop for a cyclist even if he is lying dead in the street.

You need to be lying naked in the street.

We picked ourselves up and righted the bikes. My bike was okay, but Franca's was a mess. We got our hands filthy trying to get her chain back on the spiky thing, which has a name I don't care to learn.

We succeeded but then we couldn't get the spiky thing back under the shiny thing, and I would bother to explain the problem but we all have better things to do.

Luckily, two nice men came over and asked us if we needed help. I couldn't say yes fast enough, even though they were totally married and I was rapidly concluding that falling off your bicycle isn't the way to meet single men.

And while the guys are fixing Franca's bike, lo and behold, who do we see racing down the trail but the Knight on the White Bicycle, who fixed my flat last time. I said to our two guys, "That's the guy who helped us last week," and one of the men laughed, thinking I was kidding.

I wasn't.

I watched my White Knight pedal away. I didn't chase after him or otherwise embarrass myself.

Until now.

Then one of the other men asked me, "Hey, aren't you that author, Lisa Scottoline?"

To which I answered, "No, absolutely not. Nobody as cool as Lisa Scottoline would keep falling off a bicycle. But I read her books and they're awesome. Have you bought one lately? You should."

So that's what I learned from my latest bicycle misadventure.

That this is America, and good Samaritans abound.

And if you can't sell one thing, sell another.

LIFE AMONG THE RUINS

BY FRANCESCA

I would never let a man ruin my life.

But they sure can ruin my favorite places.

For instance, there's a Mexican restaurant near me that has the best fish tacos in the city. The tacos are never soggy, they don't skimp on the guacamole, and there's nothing freaky under the fry batter.

If I could marry those fish tacos, I would.

Unfortunately, the romance of the restaurant has been ruined ever since my last boyfriend and I had the Breakup Talk there.

It's a decision I deeply regret. I should have protected the tacos.

So I made a conscious effort to go back there with a girlfriend a couple weeks later, to reverse the transformation from the Place My Boyfriend and I Broke Up back to Home of the Insane Fish Tacos.

Everything was going to plan, I could feel the bad juju dissolving like salt on a margarita glass, and at the end of dinner, I signed our check with an optimistic flourish.

Until our waiter asked for my phone number.

Flattering, but awkward. And worse? I gave it to him.

What was I thinking? Well, to be honest, he was hot *and* had an accent, so thinking was difficult — but I knew nothing about him, I wasn't going to date him. I was just vulnerable!

Clearly it's still The Place My Boyfriend and I Broke Up, and if you take me there, ply me with tequila, and tell me I'm pretty, I'm either going to cry or make out with you.

The guy did text me and I declined.

So now I definitely can never go back.

Adios, Baja Fish Tacos of my dreams. I'll see you in takeout.

Even the places with good memories of my ex — especially those places — are ruined, like our favorite brunch spot. We spent so many sunny Saturdays sitting outside with Pip, we befriended a waitress, Taylor. I could've given up the lobster egg scramble, but I couldn't give up Taylor, with her excellent service, cool side gig playing rock-cello, and fabulous lipstick colors.

Do you *know* how hard it is to find the

right red?

So I decided to rechristen it as a dinner spot. The different lighting and menu worked in my favor as I waited for my friend to arrive, but then Taylor stopped to say hi and asked how my boyfriend was doing.

I told her we broke up, but that "I'm getting custody of you in the divorce."

Truth be told, I'm lucky to have created enough good memories with someone to leave my surroundings a little altered. Past loves are allowed to ruin restaurants; they've earned that.

And I'm on a diet anyway.

But now a random man is messing with my gym, and that's unacceptable.

As you may recall, I fought for this gym membership. I worked out all summer, lost fifteen pounds, and paid enough each month to break a sweat just looking at my bank account. The perk that makes this gym worthwhile is its rooftop pool. It's my reward, my oasis, my Happy Place.

But last week, a middle-aged man in the pool chair beside me struck up some friendly small chat, and I obliged, as I would any polite stranger. And what does he do?

Gets my email address from my website and sends me sex poetry about me.

It was not flattering; it was explicit,

deluded, and disturbing.

And, in my professional opinion, very poorly written. Buddy, if you're reading this, try journaling to build your skills, and keep reading.

I was devastated to have my Happy Place turned into the Place Where Some Creep Imagined Me Naked, but autumn was around the corner.

Sir, consider yourself saved by the bell. Because next summer, I won't be so nice. The communal pool is not your Lady Hunting Ground or open mic night for your Perv Poetry Slam. Mess with me again, and see it become the Place a Five-Foot-Five Woman Told You Off and Made You Cry in Public.

You've got a second chance to stay out of my way.

Don't ruin it.

In It to Win It

BY LISA

I have a new financial plan.

I'm playing the lottery.

I don't know why I started, but it might have to do with the fact that I've been thinking about it for forty-five years.

Or the fact that some of my friends are retiring, and my retirement is now pushed back to 2022.

Meaning that I will have to be 2,022 years old to retire.

And then I happened to be driving to New York, and you can't drive anywhere without seeing those lighted-up billboards with astronomical numbers for the Powerball jackpot.

There were so many zeros, it reminded me of my marital history.

LOL.

Also, I remembered that Mother Mary always used to play the lottery and she actually won. Never the big payout, but $50 here and $100 there, just enough for me to think that I should try my luck.

So I bought my first lottery ticket on Sunday afternoon, after my bike ride, standing in line like a rookie. The lady in front of me chose her numbers, filling the circles on a sheet that reminded me of taking the SATs.

But math and I never got along, so I let the machine choose my numbers, and when the impatient clerk asked me how many tickets I wanted, I had to ask them how much it cost per ticket, and so I went whole hog for ten bucks and he gave me back a tiny piece of paper that look like a Dunkin' Donuts receipt for a cup of coffee.

I stuck it in my wallet, excited all the way home, dreaming of the things I would do with my million-dollar jackpot.

I have dreamed about winning the lottery for years, but I never actually played until now.

It's hard to win if you don't play.

Maybe that should be their new slogan?

The clerk had told me the drawing was on Wednesday night, and when I went home, I checked the website, which was cheerfully multicolored, heavy on the green, for obvious reasons.

And embarrassingly enough, I have to

admit that I counted the days until Wednesday night.

I thought the drawing was at seven, but that turns out to be one of the other lottery games because who knew there's not just one lottery game but about 3 million and they all have different rules and different times for the drawings.

Sheesh.

So when Wednesday night rolled around, I grabbed my little tickets/receipt out of my wallet and hurried to the website and waited for the minute hand to go from 10:59 to 11:00, to see the winning numbers.

Numbers appeared on the screen, five white balls with numbers and one red one, and then I looked down on my ticket and realized the problem.

I couldn't read the damn thing.

There were five lines of numbers, twenty-five numbers in all, and then the Powerball number on the far right with QP next to it, and I still don't know what QP means.

I had no idea if I had won.

I do have a modicum of common sense, so I figured that if I had a line of numbers that matched, I was $50 million richer, but then I clicked on the How to Play page, and it turns out there are about 3 billion other combinations that qualify as a winning ticket.

Who knew?

Mother Mary, undoubtedly.

I could win $1 million if I matched four white circles but not the red one, or four dollars if I matched the red circle but none of the white ones, and it was so many different permutations that I felt like I was taking the SATs again.

I couldn't figure out if I'd won anything but I couldn't bring myself to throw the ticket away, in case it was a winner.

It was a no-win situation.

And now I feel like a loser, in more ways than one.

But I'm buying another ticket.

I'm powerless over Powerball.

MY BUDDY

BY LISA

As I write this, I'm not sure whether it's going to have a happy ending or not.

Which makes it just like life.

Because last week, a little pony that I happen to love, named Buddy, took very ill with colic. Basically, colic means a bad stomachache, but if it's bad enough, like an impacted colon, it can kill him.

You didn't know I was going to say impacted colon in a humor book, did you?

If you can't identify with having a sick pony, I'm guessing you can identify with the point of this little story, which is that it's hard to give up on something you love.

Whether it has fur or not.

By the way, Buddy is thirty years old.

And just FYI, ponies can live up to thirty-five or even forty years old and beyond, so Buddy has plenty of time left.

In fact, he's only middle-aged, like me.

If fifty-nine is middle-aged.

WHICH IT IS.

In any event, one night last week, Buddy didn't eat dinner, which is not like him.

See how much we have in common?

I called the vet, who said that he had colic and that he might need surgery. So I loaded Buddy in the horse trailer and drove him over to see the geniuses at the Penn Vet's New Bolton Center. The vet on call that night was Dr. Southwood, one of the country's leading experts in colic surgery, in addition to being one of the nicest people you could ever meet. I say this because, among other reasons, when she saw a grown woman crying over a pony, she didn't point and laugh.

She recommended surgery, and the thought terrified me because I didn't think you could operate on a thirty-year-old pony. I blurted out, "But he'll die!"

To which she said, "I operate on ponies his age all the time. I don't give up on him, just because he's old."

I thought to myself, there's a lesson in that.

When bad stuff happens, I try to find the lesson in it.

If I can't find the lesson in it, I try to find the humor in it.

If I can't find the lesson or the humor in

it, it's my second marriage.

So Dr. Southwood operated on Buddy, and she saved his life. He looked pretty good for a day, but then he started to look bad and developed a different problem.

I'm trying to save you the colon talk here.

Dr. Southwood said, "I think we might have to operate again. Do I have your permission?"

I answered, "Absolutely. Don't give up on him just because he's old."

So she operated again, and saved his life again, and six days later, he's doing terrific. I visit Buddy every day in the hospital for a couple of hours, and he's a lot smaller than the fancy show horses they have at New Bolton, but he knows he's as important as they are, and he is loved.

He doesn't think he stopped counting just because he's thirty, either.

He's been fighting for his life, and right now, it looks like he's going to win.

He's still at the hospital, but he's letting me know he wants to go home by turning his feed bucket upside down and neighing at a cute little white pony across the way.

He's an aging stud.

He's the Michael Douglas of ponies.

Or the Kevin Costner.

Or the Robert Redford.

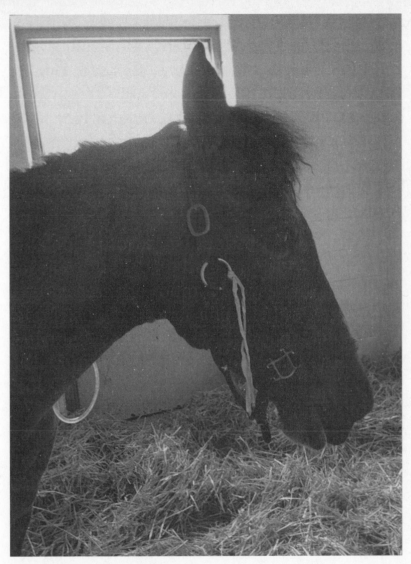

My little pony, Buddy

Or the Al Pacino.
I could go on, but you get the point.
I might be crazy, but a lot of those guys
look as good to me as they always did.

In fact, Kevin Costner looks even better.

So does Robert Redford.

To be real, Al Pacino looks worse, but he can still dance.

Buddy can't fox-trot, but he can trot.

And I'm going to make sure his stall is clean, for when he comes home.

CHECK, PLEASE?

BY FRANCESCA

The difficulty of dating in New York City is the stuff of legend. Television and film have completely contradictory takes on it, showing it to be at once incredibly easy and impossibly difficult.

They're not wrong.

The sheer volume of people allows for lots of dating interactions among wildly incompatible people. But the truth is always stranger than fiction, and the behavior I've encountered on dates makes me think that some of these men have never read a book or seen a movie in their lives.

Aliens could manage a first date better.

Let's start with appropriate topics. It's common advice to avoid hot-button issues like politics, religion, and sex on a first date. But it goes without saying that there are some subjects best left for later — or never.

I've been on two different first dates with two different men who discussed their love of enemas.

You heard me.

ENEMAS.

The first guy discussed it in context of a broader conversation of "things my ex-girlfriend introduced me to that I still enjoy," already a winning first-date topic, then he actually tried to convince me to go to his enema . . . practitioner?

Proctitioner?

"You *have* to go to my guy. He can seem shady at first, since he works out of his apartment and the place is kind of dirty, but I can vouch for him, he's the best."

He was like Yelp for your butt.

Check, please?

The next enemaniac I encountered managed to top the butt-Yelper, no pun intended. The second guy's enema practitioner was his *mother.*

Where's Sigmund Freud when you need him?

Again, my date offered this information unprompted and without reservation. I should commend him for his openness, but some doors are supposed to remain shut.

Back doors.

This was several years ago — the punchline? Mama's boy got married last month. In the pictures on Facebook, his new wife looked normal and cute.

Good luck, sweetie. Make sure he keeps the coffee cans clearly labeled.

Emily Post doesn't cover this, but I will: please don't talk about your butthole on a first date. It's unappetizing.

Which leads us to Rule Number 2: Keep it classy.

Once, I was out to drinks with a guy, and the female bartender happened to compliment me on my curly hair.

After I thanked her and she left to get our drinks, my date commented, "You must get that a lot."

"Oh, from time to time," I said, flattered. "Everyone has their good points. What is it about you that gets the most compliments?"

Without missing a beat, he answered, "My dick."

I guffawed right in his face. I thought, *this guy has great comic timing.*

However, he was not amused. "What? It's true." He looked at me like *I* was the inappropriate one.

Seriously?

Needless to say, I was no longer interested in verifying his claim.

And some people just don't know how to tell a good story. My friend says it's the writer in me that puts such importance on this, but believe me, when you're looking for someone to sit across the table from for the next fifty years, it matters.

Just last night I went on a terrible first date. There was a lot that was not ideal, but his main offense was that conversation was like pulling teeth. He began stories where they should have ended, and ended stories where they should have begun. It's hard to explain, so let me give you an example.

When he mentioned that he'd had a "crazy Sunday," I pounced on the opportunity to encourage him to speak more than a few words at a time.

"A 'crazy Sunday?' *That* sounds like a story," I said.

Boy, was it. He launched into an elaborate tale, ostensibly about a party his friend threw, but it was drowned in a sea of needless details — the names of people I don't know, the logistics of who invited who, how he came to decide to go — I struggled not to zone out. At the end of his five-minute monologue, I understood the gist was this: his buddies rented out the penthouse of the Hilton for a party that Sunday afternoon.

"Oh, that sounds nice," I said, glancing around for the waiter to rescue me from any more of this story.

"Yeah," he said, taking a sip from his water

glass. "But when I got there, it turned out to be a sex party."

This is not just burying the lede, this is dipping its feet in concrete and dumping it off the Brooklyn Bridge.

I stared at him, my eyes begging, *Go on . . .*

But he picked up the menu and began considering it, his story apparently finished, according to him.

Not to me. "Wait, what?"

He looked up from the menu, surprised. "It turned out to be a sex party," he repeated.

I laughed. "I don't know what you mean by that."

He frowned. "Well, it was a hotel suite, so there were bedrooms, and people were going in them."

"Like, couples who were already at the party together? Or couples swapping, or multiples? What are we talking about here?"

"I don't know what was going on behind those doors. I mostly saw people making out, and one man licked a woman's foot." His gaze fell back to the menu.

"Did you . . . *partake* in any of the bedrooms or the foot-licking?"

He chuckled and shook his head. "No." Again, no further detail.

All right then.

"So, do you want to share an appetizer?"

The rest of dinner was similarly unsatisfying. He didn't walk me home, although he did try to kiss me outside the restaurant (dude, that's what the walk home is for), and I left feeling frustrated. After being in a relationship for two years, I had been excited to be single again, but maybe I'd forgotten just how rough this city can be for romance. Too many women, too many options.

As I walked home, alone, it began to rain, because sometimes life really is like the movies. After the date I'd had, the only logical place to take shelter was Magnolia Bakery.

I walked up to the cupcake counter, where a female baker explained that they had three specialty flavors — caramel, pistachio, something called "Hummingbird" — she described them, each one sounding better than the next.

"Help me, I need guidance," I said, meaning it in more ways than one.

"They're all really good."

If only men were more like cupcakes.

I picked pistachio and began to vent. "I just had the worst date. Thirty-nine years old and he couldn't pick a restaurant, couldn't dress, couldn't talk — ugh."

"Oh no, boring?"

"So boring!"

She handed me the box. "Lose his number."

I laughed. "Done."

I went to pay, and a round man with a sweet face at the register said, "I'm sorry you had a bad night."

"Nothing refined sugar can't fix."

"Girl, I feel you. You doing the online thing?"

"I haven't tried that yet, does that work?"

He shuddered in reply.

Just then, the woman who helped me earlier brought a box containing the other flavored cupcakes. "On us."

"No, you're too nice!" I cried. But they made me take it, so I insisted they keep all the change, and we had a good laugh, my new friends, Brad and Yvonne.

I went home happy, reminded of why whether I'm single or not, I'm always in love with New York.

;)

BY LISA

I'm a happy person.

But you wouldn't necessarily know it from my face.

Which evidently means I'm in big trouble.

The other day, I saw an article about a study done by several psychologists who determined that we judge others based on their facial features at rest, or their "resting faces."

As soon as I saw that headline, I hoped this was going to be good news for me.

My face is always at rest.

Unfortunately, so is my body.

But the psychologists discovered something they called a "bitchy resting face," which gave me pause, as I didn't realize that "bitchy" was a psychological term.

I also wondered if men could have a "bitchy" resting face.

Or if that was simply called a "face."

But let's not get bitchy.

God forbid.

Anyway, the bottom line of the study was that people with bitchy resting faces were viewed as less trustworthy or competent. They were less likely to be hired for jobs and less likely to be voted for if they ran for office. In contrast, people whose resting face was on the smiley side were instantly viewed as more competent and trustworthy.

The psychologists called this face-ism.

So they beat me to the bad pun.

I wondered if these guys were psychologists or humorists.

Actually I think these chucklehounds were onto something, because I am the happiest person I know with the bitchiest resting face.

I found this out a few years ago, when I was being interviewed on TV about my books, and they showed me on a split screen with two other authors. I had a little earplug in my ear, and I didn't know what it was for until the interview started and somebody started yelling in my ear:

"SMILE WHEN THE OTHER AUTHORS ARE TALKING!"

So I did, looking like I had just been electrocuted but was really happy about it.

Mercifully, the segment ended, and during the commercial, the producer came up to me, and said, "You're the only author not smiling when someone else is talking."

I blinked. "That's because I listen when other people are talking."

Which was completely true, at least when I'm on television. Otherwise, when other people are talking, I'm interrupting.

The producer frowned. "So, smile when you're listening."

Now I was actually frowning. "But we're talking about murder and injustice in fiction. These are serious subjects."

"Smile anyway. It's a visual medium. If you're not smiling, people will change the channel."

The producer went away, the TV show resumed, and I tried to keep my smiley-face on while we talked about gruesome major felonies.

Needless to say, they never had me on the show again.

Because they lacked a sense of humor, which means knowing when to smile and when not to.

In any event, I'm guessing that most people I know have a bitchy resting face.

Or maybe when you get older, your face just falls into lines and everybody else thinks that's bitchy.

I have a group of great girlfriends, and I

can picture what every one of them looks like when she's listening. They look serious, caring, and thoughtful, not bitchy.

That's why they're my friends.

I challenge anybody out there with a brain to have a resting face that's anything but bitchy.

The test of this might be as close as your smartphone. Did you ever inadvertently turn on the camera function to selfie mode when you were looking down?

Yikes.

I myself have actually gasped at the sight of myself in my own phone.

I don't look bitchy, I look dead.

Or maybe I look like a dead bitch.

In truth, women my age are not taking many selfies. Most of the time we don't even want our picture taken at all. The best way to get a group of middle-aged woman to run away is to aim a camera at them.

In fact, I'm pretty sure that you could rob a bank that way.

You don't need a gun, just a smartphone.

Hold up the camera and threaten to take their picture.

"Okay, everybody say, Flee!"

It's a Miracle!

BY LISA

I'm a mystery writer, but now I have a real-life mystery to solve:

There are three cats in my house.

Which one is peeing in my bedroom?

Where is Nancy Drew when you need her?

By the way, if you don't want to hear about wee-wee, read no further.

But if you, like me, are plagued by the problems of the pets that purport to love you, come along for the ride.

Bring your own blue roadster, like the Girl Detective.

You won't need a magnifying glass, but a roll of paper towels and a jug of Nature's Miracle would come in handy.

If you don't know what Nature's Miracle is, you've come to the right place.

If you ask me, Nature's Miracle is Chocolate Cake.

But that's not the kind of Nature's Miracle to which I'm referring.

It's not as if I'm capitalizing things for fun, though capitalizing things is fun for writers.

Ours is a quiet life.

By way of background, I own three cats, all of which lead complicated lives.

Vivi is a gray cat who is adorable, but has intimacy issues, and as such, has nothing to do with me. She lives in the dining room, which I never use, so it's blocked off by a gate, which prevents the dogs from bothering her.

Mimi is a friendly black-and-white tuxedo cat, who has since moved with Daughter Francesca to Manhattan, because that's where you live if you're wearing a permanent tuxedo.

Spunky is a tan, long-haired cat, whom I adopted after my beloved next-door neighbor Harry died, and there was no one to take in his cat. I thought that he was going to die any second.

That was five years ago.

No one knows exactly how old Spunky is, and I thought he was sixteen.

I think he's three.

I will be dead before this cat dies.

Be that as it may, because I thought Spunky was in his dotage and deserved a quiet life, maybe even quieter than mine, I put him and his litter box in Francesca's room, so that he would be completely out of the way and could sail off into the sunset.

So anyway, last week, Francesca came home to visit, bringing Mimi, and the three cats had the run of the second floor.

In short order, I began to notice puddles in the corner of my bedroom, then in the corner of Francesca's bedroom, and finally in the corner of my office.

In short, this is disgusting.

So I cleaned up the cat pee, then started pouring Nature's Miracle on top of the stain, because Nature's Miracle is something that is supposed to remove the smell of urine.

But the thing is, Nature's Miracle smells like urine.

Either that, or it doesn't work.

This would be a distinction without a difference.

In the end, I'm guessing that the shame is on me. I might be the only person in the world who buys a product that bills itself as a miracle and expects it to work.

Do miracles exist?

In my life, the only miracle I've ever experienced is divorce.

But to stay on point, maybe this isn't the fault of Nature's Miracle, a thought that leads me, by my powers of deduction, to a darker truth:

When a cat pees somewhere, it's going to stink to high heaven no matter what you spray it with, including Febreeze, Lysol, or Chanel No. 5, all of which I tried, in that order.

Then, after I cleaned all the cat pee and doused it with an allegedly miraculous product, I tried to figure out which cat was the culprit.

They weren't talking.

I tried closing various doors and putting up different gates, then observing which cat did its business in which corner, but they outsmarted me.

Because I sleep at night, and they don't.

Next, I bought new litter boxes and put them in the corners of my bedroom, Francesca's bedroom, and my office, trying to beat them at their own game.

But one of them, or all of them, peed *beside* the litter boxes.

So I cleaned up the mess again, doused it with you-know-what again, and closed the doors to my bedroom, Francesca's bedroom, and my office.

Now I walk around my house as if I live in a hotel, with all the doors shut.

Who dun it?

I Want What I Want

BY LISA

A fun thing about being single is that you can reverse man-shop.

By which I mean, until I find a man I want to be with, I like to pick out men I *don't* want to be with.

I call it The Better Off Dead Game, but it could just as easily be called The Better Off Celibate Game.

Of course, celibacy is not as bad as death, but they are related concepts. As in, I'm dead below the waist, but on the bright side, I can still watch TV.

Anyway, no matter what you call the game, I play it all the time, which might be why I spend my Saturday nights with dogs.

Like the other day, I was in New York, where Francesca, Laura, and I had a meeting with our wonderful publisher Jen, after which we went to a bar to have a celebratory drink. Francesca and Jen ordered wine, but I had just turned in the manuscript of my next book and had been dreaming of a margarita, so I ordered it as soon as I sat down. So did Laura.

Nevertheless, the bartender handed us drinks menus. "Ladies, we have great specialty drinks you should try. I recommend the Sofia."

I didn't open the drinks menu. "Thanks but I'm dying for that margarita."

Laura said, "Me, too."

Jen and Francesca chimed in, "We'll have the wine."

The bartender frowned. "You didn't even look at the drinks menu."

I said, "I know, I want a margarita."

The bartender kept frowning. "At least look at the drinks menu."

So I did, God knows why, but I couldn't read it without my reading glasses, and neither could Laura. Plus we both wanted a margarita, so we asked for one a third time.

At which point the bartender asked, "You're *really* not going to try the Sofia?"

I answered, firmly, "No, can we please have our drinks?"

He went away, scowling.

And I knew I was Better Off Dead.

Hell, I was even Better Off Celibate.

See? It's a fun game, right?

But wait, there's more.

It was a quiet Sunday morning, and I was riding my bicycle on the trail with Franca. The trail was hardly crowded except for a few other people riding bikes, walking, or jogging together.

Suddenly a man with two small kids started yelling at us, "You should ride single file! You should be riding single file!"

I didn't understand what his problem was, because we were nowhere near him or the kids. Franca and I are insanely obsequious on the trail, always riding single file when it gets busy, letting people go ahead of us, and generally being Codependents on Wheels.

Most of the time, we're just trying to stay upright and not crash anymore.

So I called back to him, nicely, "Don't worry, we'll go single file if somebody else comes the other way."

The man yelled back, "You should ride single file ALL THE TIME!"

But we kept rolling, and he kept yelling at us, then he switched to yelling at the next twosome who rode by.

Yikes.

Wanna play?

Better Off Watching TV.

In fact, Better Off Watching Infomercials.

To my thinking, both of these guys are really the same type of guy, a variation of

Mr. Take Charge. And I always liked that kind of guy when I was younger. I wanted a guy who had all the answers, handled any situation, and basically was a combination of Daddy, Superman, and Bradley Cooper.

This last because, are you blind?

And honestly, I don't think it's Mr. Take Charge's fault that he takes charge, because just as I got the message that that was what I was supposed to want, I suspect he got the message that was what he was supposed to be.

Or maybe what happens is that Mr. Take Charge stays the same, but the women change, like I did.

We grow up, if we're lucky.

We get older and realize we don't need adult supervision.

We are the adult supervision.

And as I got older, I realized that Mr. Take Charge morphs into Mr. Control Freak.

And probably from there into Mr. Ray Rice.

It's taken me decades to figure out exactly what I want, and to be able to ask for it.

And it's not Mr. Take Charge.

It's a margarita.

No more Mrs. Nice Guy.

THE MUTUAL FADE-OUT
BY FRANCESCA

I just pulled off the greatest trick of any dater: the mutual fade-out.

This is the holy grail of the socially anxious. The royal flush of the reluctant in romance. The *coup de grâce* of the co-dependents.

For those who aren't familiar, a fade-out is when you're dating someone who you don't want to see anymore, so you just gradually stop returning their calls and texts until they give up on you. No explanation, no honesty, no opportunity for personal growth, no closure, just . . . a relationship fade to black. It's the path-of-least-resistance method of breaking things off. It's cowardly, really.

That's why people love to do it.

But the mutual fade-out is the only way to get away with the blow-off guilt-free, because you both do it to each other at exactly the same time.

I thought it was urban legend.

In the past, I've resisted the siren song of the fade-out. The thought of leaving a guy wondering what happened and feeling bad about himself gives the codependent in me a cold sweat, so I've always forced myself to offer a tactfully vague goodbye.

Of course, my penchant for half honesty has blown back in my face plenty of times.

I once texted a guy after a second date that I really loved meeting him but I thought we'd be better as friends.

He wrote back: "Yeah right. Why don't you just be honest and say you never want to see me again?"

Um, because I'm not an animal, sir.

See, that was someone I should've faded out.

When I'm truly honest, they complain about that, too. There was one guy who drank way too much when out with me and a bunch of his buddies. After returning from the bathroom to find me chatting with his friends, he hooked his arm around my neck and accused me of flirting with his bros. Then he bent me down into a headlock right in the middle of the bar and slurred into my ear:

"Were you talking about how fat I am?

Are you saying, 'you gotta get him to the gym?' "

I'd never had a guy get physical with me before, but I wasn't about to let myself be victimized, especially not over some dude's lame body issues. I broke free and stormed out.

Headlocks are a deal breaker, and while I would've been more than justified in using the fade-out on this guy, I wanted him to know never to contact me again. So I emailed him a short, civil, note that said, "After your behavior last night, I don't feel comfortable moving forward in our relationship. I have no hard feelings, and I wish you well."

Well.

He saw my one paragraph and raised me six. He replied with an epic email detailing what a snob I was, how he "expected more" from me, that I could "at least treat him with a bit more respect" and explain myself. He conceded that his behavior "may have been immature, brutish, and insensitive," but claimed it wasn't nearly as callous — if he knew a word that big — as my refusal to give him a chance to "learn from [his] mistakes."

It ended with a final paragraph written entirely in the third person: "I'm sorry

Francesca Serritella from Philadelphia thinks she's too good to get to know [Idiot's Name Redacted] from Long Island, New York."

[Idiot's Name Redacted] should be the title of my future romantic memoirs.

So there are pitfalls to being a straight shooter, but in general I think it's the right thing to do.

Unfortunately, I'm out of practice.

So recently, when things fizzled with this guy I'd been seeing, I was dreading breaking the news to him.

And lo and behold, the mutual fade-out appeared to save the day.

He and I both slowly fell off each other's planets at exactly the same time.

It's pretty much the best ever. No awkward conversation. No hurt feelings. No problem.

I pulled it off almost by accident. Looking at our stats, I was on the fence about whether I could get away with a fade-out. We had been on six dates, which is right on the borderline for blow-offs, but, because I was traveling a lot, our relationship was spread out over a couple months, which points to a phone call, at least. I was going to bite the bullet, I just hadn't gotten around to it.

While I was procrastinating, it dawned on me — hey, I haven't heard from him either.

Thing is, I'm kind of surprised. I thought he liked me. I thought it was only me who didn't like him. I thought telling him I didn't want to see him again would hurt his feelings.

So it's good that it was mutual, of course.

Because I didn't *not* like him. I simply began to think we were too different, and the fragile bubble of my crush had popped. The truth is, I might've given him one more chance.

Just to be polite.

I knew we weren't going to work out in the long haul. He'd flaked out on me on our penultimate date, canceling our Friday night plans at 6:30 P.M., *after* making *me* get in touch with *him* to confirm. Six-thirty is too late to cancel on a weekend night; I thought it was rude and unreliable. So that was the beginning of the end for me.

But wait.

What if his flaking out was the beginning of the end for him?

That would mean his beginning began before mine.

Maybe when I thought I was giving him a second chance, he was already giving me my third.

Even so, when I said goodbye to him after our last date a week ago, I knew that it would be the last time I'd see him.

I just hope *he* knows that.

You didn't fire me, I quit.

The other night, I had a dream where I saw him at a party. He was in a full-body cast, complete with a halo brace, and he was deeply apologetic that he hadn't been in touch:

"I would've called, if it weren't for the accident . . ."

I'm glad to know that my subconscious has such great self-esteem.

Although also in my dream, I rebuffed him when he asked me out.

Yes, dream-me broke up with a man after an accident that put him in a body cast.

Less glad to know that my subconscious is a heartless bitch.

But I guess that proves it, I really don't want to see him again. And apparently he doesn't want to see me either. And nobody got hurt. The technicality of who dumped who doesn't matter in the slightest.

Who cares?

Not me.

Moving on.

(Are you buying any of that?)

Ugh. See? This is why I don't do the fade-out.

THE GOOD WIFE OR THE DUMB WIFE?

BY LISA

Things just got real for the Real Housewives.

As you may have heard, Joe Giudice and his wife, Teresa, who is one of the *Real Housewives of New Jersey* on Bravo TV, are going to jail for bankruptcy fraud.

I'm going to miss Teresa, whose lack of anger management was a thing of beauty. She famously turned over a table in anger, and I don't know a single woman in the world who hasn't dreamed of doing that, or at least being the kind of woman who would do that, on impulse.

By the way, when she flipped the table, she yelled "prostitution whore," which is a great thing to yell at any time.

Try it and see.

At home.

Not in the library.

Everybody made fun of Teresa because it wasn't the most literate phrase, but to be

271

fair, English isn't her first language, and in any event, you need to have fun in life. So when you're about to turn over a table in a blind rage, feel free to scream whatever noun combination you can come up with.

For example, flip a table and yell "bankruptcy fraud."

It's fun.

I also think Teresa and Joe deserve to go to jail for Perpetuating Italian-American Stereotypes. I'm proud of my Italian-American heritage, which is as plain as the nose on my face.

Mother Mary always liked to say that we got more oxygen than anybody else in the room.

She's always with me in spirit, especially when I breathe in.

Anyway, I hate it when an Italian-American does something bad, whether it's a crime like bankruptcy fraud or a simple error in judgment, like not marrying me.

I'm talking to you, Al Pacino, Robert De-Niro, and Bradley Cooper, whose mother is Italian-American.

For us, that counts.

In fact, if you like Italian food, you're Italian to us.

We're liberal in our interpretation.

We take all comers.

Especially Bradley Cooper.

Also we need new team members.

To replace the ones who go to jail.

Just kidding.

Anyway, I cringed when I saw that Joe Giudice had committed tax fraud, because it was a trend that Al Capone started, and people are going to get the idea that Italian-Americans don't pay their taxes, which will mean that they think I don't pay my taxes, and I will never get the credit I deserve for paying every last penny and then some.

I pay my taxes, people.

Finally, I admit, I feel bad for the true victims of the Giudices, their four young daughters. It's never a good thing when mom is going to jail for over a year and dad for about four years. The court staggered their sentences, so that Teresa can go to jail after Christmas, and then her husband will serve his time after she returns.

You might think the timing is a sweet deal, granted because of their TV fame, and you might be right.

So Bravo!

I watched Teresa being interviewed on TV last night with her husband, Joe, and her defense was that she signed whatever he put in front of her without reading it first.

Was she The Good Wife?

Or The Dumb Wife?

As a result, she's no longer a Housewife.

To be honest, she is not the first woman who has made that mistake.

I've even done it, and I'm a lawyer.

So ladies, have we learned our lesson?

I have.

We don't want to be seen as Only The Wife anymore, and we can't have it both ways.

We can live blissfully, just not blissfully ignorant.

TROUBLEMAKER

BY LISA

Well, that settles it.

I'm not moving to China.

You probably read last week about Guo Yushan, a Chinese man who was arrested there, for breaking the country's law against "picking quarrels and provoking troubles."

Yikes.

Somebody needs to stop sweating the small stuff.

Lighten up, China.

I can't imagine making a law against picking quarrels and provoking troubles. I don't think life is worth living if you can't pick a quarrel or provoke troubles, from time to time.

In fact, I was raised to pick quarrels and provoke troubles.

Mother Mary specialized in picking quarrels and provoking troubles.

I remember the time I ordered her a crossword puzzle jar from the *New York*

Times, but it never got delivered to her. She raised holy hell with the *New York Times* itself.

The Gray Lady was no match for my gray lady.

I wouldn't want to live in a country in which nobody picks quarrels or provokes troubles.

First, there would be no lawyers.

Okay, maybe that's a bad argument.

Please don't think I'm making fun of the Chinese situation, because I'm just trying to find the humor in it, which is exactly what Mr. Guo did himself, before he was arrested. He predicted his own arrest because, two years ago, he had helped his friend, a blind legal activist, escape to the United States with his family.

So Mr. Guo knew he'd get in trouble for making trouble.

Because, under Chinese law, that's the same thing as helping your friend.

Who just happens to be blind.

I'm pretty sure the Chinese government must have a heart, but I'm not sure exactly where.

I'm guessing they kick puppies in their spare time.

Seeing Eye puppies.

But to be fair to China, the world abounds

with people who wish you would just Sit Down and Shut Up, and some of those people make their way to the top of companies.

Like Microsoft.

I'm referring to Mr. Satya Nadella, who recently advised female employees in the tech industry not to ask for raises. He said, "It's not really about asking for the raise, but knowing and having faith that the system will actually give you the right raises as you go along. It's good karma. It will come back."

In other words, ladies, don't pick quarrels.

Don't make trouble.

Sit down and shut up, and the system will reward you.

Is there any woman in the world who believes this is a good way to operate, in any area of her life, on any planet in this or any other galaxy?

Honestly, I tried that and it doesn't work.

Mr. Nadella also said, "That's the kind of person that I want to trust, that I want to give more responsibility to."

Of course, as soon as he said this, any woman worth her ovaries threw a fit, so he later apologized for being "inarticulate."

I disagree.

I think he was articulate, and he said

exactly what he thinks, and I don't accept his apology.

You can't apologize for being sexist.

The only thing he's sorry for is that he said it out loud, to a roomful of people with ears.

And ovaries.

What scares me is that his attitude isn't unique to him, CEOs, or even men, but there are plenty of women who feel the same way.

I myself was one of them.

I was a good girl, who did all the homework and got good grades, so I naturally assumed that if I kept quiet and kept doing well, success would follow.

I learned the hard way that it doesn't.

That you not only have to ask for what you want, but if they don't give it to you, you have to go out and get it, all by yourself.

Bring a club, so that you can bonk it on the head and drag it home, if that's what it takes.

And by the way, it might take years to get what you want, but don't be patient.

On the contrary, be impatient.

Ask, then demand, and if you have to, get out your club.

Karma might work, but it takes too long, and why wait?

These are the things I taught myself,
because I had simply forgotten the lesson
that Mother Mary used to say to me, which
isn't exactly sweet and motherly-sounding,
but is profoundly true:

She always said, "Lisa, don't take any
crap."

Only she didn't say "crap."

Because she was cooler than that.

Mother Mary would not have done well
in China.

God bless her.

Seeing Ghosts

BY FRANCESCA

Last night, I ran into my ex-boyfriend's best friend while on a date with someone new.

This wasn't a passing glance or a casual bump on the sidewalk; this was a full-on meet-and-greet. We were at a Brooklyn biergarten, and I had just put my purse down on the chair when I locked eyes with the person sitting at the very next table.

"Hey!" I cried, sounding like someone calling for help.

"Francesca!" He mirrored my expression of shock and fear.

But we hugged — I was with my ex for two years, so his friends had become my friends, too, and although I relinquished any claim on them now, I still had genuine affection for this guy. I just wished I'd run into him at any other time than this.

After making rapid, anxious small chat, my ex's friend introduced me to his three pals, which meant I had to introduce him to my date. As they shook hands, I could feel my smile twitching.

"Well, it was *so* good to see you!" I grabbed my date by the arm and wheeled him away.

"You don't want to sit with your friend?" he asked in my ear.

"Nope." I didn't know how to explain it further without sounding preoccupied with my ex, and I didn't want my date to feel as awkward as I did.

We sat farther away, but over my date's shoulder, I could see my ex's friend sneaking glances in our direction.

Or maybe I was the one glancing at him.

Eventually, my date decided to sit beside me for a cuddle, and I realized two things, 1) we were now in full view of their table, and 2) I could no longer hide my discomfort.

I didn't want my date to think he was the problem, so I spoke the words that never need explanation to a man:

"Let's get out of here."

Misleading, perhaps, but it got us out of there without finishing the beers.

When I told my mom and my friends the story the next day, the general take was: awesome! And some petty part of me did enjoy it. Running into your ex's friend has all the envy-inducing benefits of seeing your actual ex with none of the pathos. If I had to be seen by a member of the enemy camp, at least I was wearing a red dress, with a tall, well-built guy on a Saturday night.

If we were keeping score, I was up one.

But it didn't feel like a win. Seeing the ex-friend that night threw me off my game. He didn't fit into the version of my life I was trying to create with this new person. He was a reminder of the past, a ghost, and I wanted to feel carefree and open to indulge in the heady promise of potential.

And I definitely didn't want to think of my ex out with a new girl.

When a chapter of our life ends, we want the metaphor to be made literal. We want to turn the page and leave the past behind, completely. But that's not possible.

Not in a small town like New York.

Even without physically seeing an ex, we have Facebook and Instagram to sprinkle breadcrumbs of past loves, leading us backwards instead of forward. Before I ran into his friend, I had avoided my ex's social-media presence completely and without effort. But afterwards, I found myself creeping online.

The next morning he posted a picture with the friend I ran into. I wondered if he told him. I wondered if I wanted him to.

In other pictures, I saw he attended a friend's wedding, one that we had both been invited to before we broke up. He had told me to put it in my calendar, but I hadn't. I remembered wishing otherwise but knowing that we weren't going to make it to summer.

Now, I couldn't stop myself from combing through the photos, scanning for him, reading into body language, trying to see if he'd brought a new plus one.

It didn't look like he had, I thought, with too much relief.

You want to move on from your old life, but you don't want it to move on from you.

Past lives stubbornly live on in art. I write about past and present relationships often. But for the first time, it's a fair fight. My ex is an artist himself, a musician. It's been five months since we broke up, and although we didn't end on bad terms, we haven't seen or spoken to each other since. Now, all of a sudden, I feel a fleeting urge to go to one of his shows.

I'm not really sure what I'd seek to accomplish by doing so. In my fantasy, I don't go to the show to reopen any doors, or even to get an ill-advised drink with him afterwards. I simply feel a wish to go by myself, listen, then leave.

"So then why go at all?" my best friend asked when I confessed my thoughts to her.

I'm not really sure. Maybe to spook him. Maybe to spook myself.

"I guess I just want to listen to the music. Look for signs of happiness, of sadness."

Look for signs of me.

But I probably won't go.

Because as hard as it is to accept that the ghosts of our past linger in our lives and surroundings, it's even harder to accept when they leave no trace at all.

QUARANTINE ME

BY LISA

Today we're talking quarantine.

In short, I'm in favor.

Quarantine me.

You know, of course, I'm talking about the recent Ebola epidemic, and it goes without saying that this epidemic is horrific and terrifying. My heart goes out to anyone in the world who has lost someone they loved due to this dreaded disease. And my prayers are with anyone who has contracted Ebola. And thank God for the doctors, nurses, and others who are going over to West Africa to fight the epidemic, because they are true heroes.

As I say, all of this goes without saying.

Still, I'm saying it.

Why?

First, because I'm a mother, and as you know, it's our job to say things that go without saying. For example, for years I have been saying to Daughter Francesca:

When it's cold out, take a jacket.

I said this to her when she was eight, and I say it to her now that she's twenty-eight.

Also, I still tell her, Eat your vegetables.

You know what's funny about that?

She's a vegetarian.

Maybe she listened?

So, when I read in the newspaper that an American doctor had returned from treating Ebola patients in West Africa, then decided to eat a meatball sandwich in a restaurant, then take the subway, and then go bowling, I instantly texted Francesca, who lives in New York. I said to her what goes without saying:

Don't take the subway.

Don't go bowling.

Don't eat meatball sandwiches.

Never mind that I can't remember the last time Francesca ate a meatball sandwich, especially now that she's a vegetarian.

Also I doubt that she has ever gone bowling, but you never know, the idea to go bowling could just randomly pop into her head, and as a mother, I had to nip that in the bud. Plus she takes the subway all the time, a fact I hated way before Ebola-bearing doctors started riding around.

So being a good mother, I texted her the things that went without saying. I give myself credit for not texting her the things that I really wanted to say, which were:

Come home now.

Don't touch anything in New York.

Avoid using the letter E altogether.

To stay on point about Ebola, I'm making a big point of saying what goes without saying because I know what a lot of you are going to say because of what I'm about to say next.

Which is that I'm in favor of quarantining for three weeks any health-care worker who has treated Ebola patients in West Africa.

Don't think that I'm being hysterical about Ebola. I know that it isn't easy to spread. And I'm not being mean about these health-care workers, because as I said above, I believe they are true heroes.

But everything is a cost-benefit analysis.

And in this case, the cost is me getting a dreaded disease or you staying home for three weeks.

Guess which I choose.

My answer is informed not only by the fact that I think I'm adorable, but also by the fact that I don't think being quarantined is the worst thing in the world.

I would love being quarantined.

It would be like a permanent snow day.

I wouldn't have to go out to run errands

and I might not even get out of bed. I would just watch TV or read. I could have someone deliver me my groceries. I would finally organize my closet.

In fact, I already live in quarantine.

All writers do.

I'm always inside, especially when it's cold outside.

Brrrrr.

Also, inside is all the food I like to eat, right in my very own refrigerator.

I could wait three weeks to go bowling.

And I don't eat meatball sandwiches because I'm a vegetarian, too.

But a lot of people don't like the idea of quarantine, and someone made the point that quarantine would be a hardship for returning health-care workers because they would be unable to make a living for three weeks.

Good point.

So I propose that the government pay them to stay home.

And if the government won't pay them, I will.

Because they need to earn a living, and I need to keep on living.

Living, all around, for everyone!

And no bowling until Ebola's in the gutter.

Keeping Abreast

BY LISA

I saw in the newspaper that some genius conducted a study on what constitutes the perfect female breast.

Oh, good.

They decided that the perfect breast has a 45:55 ratio, and if you're wondering what that means, it is the "ratio of the upper to the lower pole of the breast."

These people might be crazy.

If you have poles in your breasts, you're in big trouble.

But the way they describe it, the nipple is the dividing line between "the upper and lower poles." So in a breast with a 45:55 ratio, 45 percent of the breast is above the nipple, or the upper pole, and 55 percent is below the nipple, or the lower pole.

If you ask me, these people are splitting hairs.

Nipple hairs.

By the way, they conducted the study by

showing one thousand three hundred people pictures of breasts.

I wonder how much they paid the people to look at breasts all day.

Or if the people paid them to look at breasts all day.

Because the one thing that's true in this world is that people never, ever get sick of looking at breasts.

Generally speaking, men look at them because they're sexy, and women look at them to compare them to their own.

This means that after looking at breasts, one group will feel really great, and the other will feel really crummy.

Breasts have made tons of money for magazines, websites, restaurants, and beer companies. In fact, there is probably no company on earth that has not used breasts to sell something.

Breasts are busy.

And they work for almost nothing.

Of course they do, they're female.

By the way, of the one thousand three hundred people in the perfect-breast survey, 53 of them were plastic surgeons.

This surprises me.

I would have expected all one thousand three hundred to be plastic surgeons.

Because if I made my living out of making

human beings look perfect, I'd make damn sure that I got on the Perfection Committee.

The funny thing is that if you were a girl growing up a while ago — let's say you were born in 1955, hypothetically speaking — you had no idea what breasts looked like.

Okay, I'm talking about myself, really.

When I was little, the only way to see breasts was in *Playboy,* and you better believe we didn't have any of those magazines around the house.

Mother Mary didn't approve.

But when I was fourteen, I started babysitting, which was the same age I discovered *Playboy,* because I found it accidentally on purpose, in the bedroom drawers of the couple I was sitting for, after the baby was in bed.

Sorry, unnamed people.

Anyway, I looked at the breasts in *Playboy* magazine, and all of those breasts were perfect.

Perfectly large.

I don't know what the poles or ratios were, but all I knew was that when I got breasts, I wanted them to look exactly like that.

Of course, when they didn't, I felt inferior.

I assumed everybody else got the good breasts and that all of the good breasts looked exactly alike.

It took me a long time to figure out that everybody's breasts were different.

Like until last year.

And I didn't realize that *everything* about everybody's breasts was different, whether it was shape, nipple size or color, or anything like that. Nor did I realize that breasts change with time, and gravity, so that even if they were perfect once, they won't be perfect forever.

Because breasts are no different from every other part of your body, which is different from everybody else's parts, all of which change over time, and it generally ain't for the better.

But for some reason, women still want to be perfect.

Whatever that is.

And it's not only breasts.

Nowadays it's faces, too, and we're flocking to plastic surgeons and paying them to inject and fill and puff our cheeks and lips, too, so that we all look completely alike, evidently closer to the ideal.

Which is a fish.

To be precise, a very young fish.

So, in my opinion, what constitutes the perfect female breast?

Answer: Whatever you've got on your chest.

If it's little or if it's big, if it's flat or if it's skinny, if it's old or if it's young, no matter what it is, it's perfect.

If you have two breasts, that's perfect.

If you have one, that's perfect.

And if you've had breast cancer and had your breast reconstructed, it's perfect.

And if you had breast cancer and decided not to have your breast reconstructed, that's perfect, too.

Why?

Because you're alive.

Because you're an individual, and as such, unique.

And because nobody's perfect.

At least nobody human.

IF I WERE BEYONCÉ

BY FRANCESCA

Beyoncé is the spiritual leader of our time. She's like Oprah if Oprah could twerk. And while her wisdom reaches from big topics like feminism all the way to not being ready for this jelly, Beyoncé has helped me most with solving problems of the heart.

When I couldn't get my first boyfriend to say those three little words after a year of dating, he could at least put "Crazy in Love" on a mix CD.

Yes, kids, in my day, people listened to music via a saucer called a compact disc. And we walked six miles to school.

When my college sweetheart and I broke up in a fiery argument, he tried to get the last word by leaving a shoebox of my belongings outside my door the next morning, including such precious items as bobby pins, a hair elastic, and one plastic earring.

I thought, is this your, "Everything I own in a box to the left?" Are you trying to out-

Beyoncé me? Please.

I'd already made "Irreplaceable" my new ringtone as soon as I left his dorm room.

But this most recent breakup had no pyrotechnics. To quote a poet nearly as popular as Beyoncé, we went out not with a bang, but with a whimper.

My birthday and our anniversary fell on the same day. We had planned to have a special dinner and exchange gifts. I had gotten his anniversary gift months earlier and kept it hidden in my closet, counting down the days until I got to give it to him. But when the day came, he had nothing for me. He was very sorry but didn't have much of an explanation. He'd been really busy. He's no good at picking out gifts. There was bad traffic that day.

It was so difficult for me to process and acknowledge that he didn't think about me the way I thought about him, that I spent that night, my birthday, consoling him for his oversight. I still tried to fix things for another month.

After we broke up, I wondered why it had taken me so long to see the ways our relationship was uneven, and worse, why it took even longer for me to recognize that unevenness as a reason to leave.

My default is to assume I don't deserve

all that much, because I don't *need* all that much. But need and deserve are two different things. Theoretically, I know I deserve good treatment, but in practice, I often feel guilty asking for things.

I never hold the men I date to the same expectations that I hold myself to. I go above and beyond for the person I love, but I don't expect or demand that in return.

That would be high-maintenance. That would be too much to ask.

But that wouldn't be too much for Beyoncé to ask. Beyoncé understands that if she gives her all, she can expect the same in return. She needs someone who puts her "Love on Top."

Top, top, top, top, to-op.

And yes, I can do all the key changes (and the runs).

And I thought of another song, Beyoncé's 2008, double-platinum hit, "If I Were a Boy." In the song, Bey imagines herself as a man, first to indulge in all the perks of boys-will-be-boys behavior, but then vows that she would be better because she knows what it's like to be on the other side.

So I put myself in the shoes of my ideal man — not some Mr. Big fantasy, but a good man, an equal partner, the type of boyfriend I would be if I were a boy. And

What would Beyoncé do?

thinking of it that way, my next step was clear:

I needed to buy myself a birthday/breakup gift.

And it had better be sparkly.

I took my best friend to the jewelry store

My mom and me at Beyoncé's concert/group therapy session

to help me choose it, to get a female opinion. We settled on a necklace with a short chain and a wide, horizontal pendant — it looked tribal and strong, and in fourteen-karat gold, it complemented my skin tone.

Well, technically it's only gold-plate, but I won't know the difference.

And I pinky-swore my friend that if I backslid with my ex, I'd have to give the necklace away and take the loss.

Six months later, I still have my necklace.

And every time I wear it, I'm reminded

that I deserve a man who can care for me at least as well as I can care for myself.

Or better.

Because that's what Beyoncé would want.

Hot Mama

BY LISA

I have met the love of my life, and it comes in a box.

I'm talking, of course, about ThermaCare.

For those of you who have yet to fall in love, allow me to explain.

ThermaCare is a heat wrap you can buy in a drugstore. It has some kind of black pods attached to a piece of paper, and you stick the paper on various parts of your body that happen to be aching, like your lower back.

Me!

In no time, the black pods start to heat up and your lower back will not only stop aching, but start feeling loose, relaxed, and ready to twerk.

Okay, I'm exaggerating, but the bottom line is, you'll feel better.

While you werk.

At least, I sure do.

Of course, this isn't a scientific explanation of what makes the wraps get hot. I didn't know what was inside the black pods, but so I could be your faithful reporter, I looked it up on the website, and it is evidently pods of iron that begin to oxidize when they hit the air, emitting a low level of heat.

As far as I'm concerned, the black pods could be magic.

Black magic.

I started using the wraps when my lower back started hurting, and the one for your back is like a superwide paper that fits around your waist and has heating pods on the back. You can wear it under your clothes all day, like the unsexiest undergarment on the planet.

Think of it as a chastity belt for your back.

It's hot, but not in a good way.

You can also wear it to bed at night and you'll drift into a toasty slumber. Plus you'll save money because you'll never have to turn the heat on. Your dogs will cuddle up to you, because you are the new furnace.

If you get hot flashes, you might start a fire.

Don't ask me how your husband, wife, or significant other will react.

My guess is they'll want one of their own.

I suppose a heating pad would do the

same thing, but you can't wear a heating pad to the supermarket and have a telltale slip of paper peeking out from underneath your shirt.

They have ThermaCare for aching knees, elbows, joints, wrists, shoulders, and "multipurpose muscle."

Luckily, none of my muscles are multipurpose.

They have only one purpose.

Which is to relax.

They also have ThermaCare for menstrual cramps, which makes me wish I still had my period.

Just kidding.

And by the way, please don't write me an angry email saying that I'm shilling for a product. I didn't get any money to write this, and I wouldn't accept any. I'm writing this out of love for ThermaCare.

I Care about ThermaCare.

Why?

Because now I'm an addict.

I started using it about a month ago, only at night, and now I have it on continuously. I started out with the heat wraps that last for eight hours but graduated quickly to the ones that last sixteen. They're expensive, but no junkie complains about the price of heroin.

There are only twenty-four hours in a day, but if you wear two wraps that last sixteen hours apiece, you have the luxury of changing your wrap before your initial high begins to wear off.

The more you have, the more you want.

I sense that I'm not the only addict, because if you look at the frequently asked questions on the ThermaCare website, one was, "How many heat wraps can I use at one time?"

Answer: You can wear more than one, but not in the same location.

Damn.

In other words, if you wrap two around your back, you might spontaneously combust.

You have to be ThermaCareful.

Princess Lisa

BY LISA

I live a fairytale existence.

But not in a good way.

When I was little, I remember reading old-school fairytales, and there was one in which every time a princess spoke, no words came out of her mouth, but only snakes, newts, spiders, and mice.

Well, it turns out that princess is me.

And they're not coming out of my mouth, but they're coming out of my heat vents.

Or from under couches.

Or even from my oven.

I don't know where to begin the fairytale.

Maybe just to remind you that every year in the autumn, I always have an invasion of wolf spiders.

To be fair, they don't invade. They have better manners than that.

They merely wait for the front door to open and run in, usually in a flying wedge.

There are NFL teams that don't have the

304

formations of these spiders.

Mine are professional spiders.

I can't bring myself to kill them, so I try to catch them under drinking glasses, flip the glasses upside down, and throw them back outside.

I've made my peace with the spiders, as I have with the mice that tend to appear this time of year, too.

I found one in the oven last week, and he wasn't helping with the cooking.

So I set a bunch of mousetraps, because I don't cut mice the same slack that I cut spiders.

You have to draw the line somewhere.

Anybody who has had a mouse in the house knows that the best and worst sound is a snap of the trap.

Then a few days ago I noticed a horrible smell coming from the wall of my bedroom closet and all the dogs were going crazy every night, at bedtime. When I couldn't take the stench anymore, I called a contractor. The dogs told him exactly where in the wall to dig.

They're cadaver dogs.

Kind of.

Anyway, in five minutes, the contractor had opened the wall and found three dead mice.

Presumably they were not blind.

Still, I can live even with dead mice.

I'm not a picky woman, and everybody's just looking to keep warm for the winter, myself included.

But just now, I was at my desk working on the computer when I happened to look down and see something dark, long, and skinny wiggling rapidly across the rug.

All the dogs were asleep.

Thanks, freeloaders.

But to stay on point, at first I thought it was a worm, but it was moving way too fast, and my body shuddered instantly, because it figured out what the thing was before my brain did.

A baby snake.

I jumped up and said, eeeeek!

Because I'm entitled.

I ran to get a glass, returned to my office, and put the glass down in front of the baby snake, who undulated cooperatively inside.

Yes!

I mean yesssssss!

Then I ran outside with the glass and left the snake in the backyard.

So he could be a snake in the grass.

It seemed only natural that there should be a living cliché in the backyard of a writer.

I thought it was over until this morning,

when I saw another baby snake crawling out of my heating vent in the floor.

Eeeeeekkkkk!

And now enough is enough.

I can put up with spiders and mice, but I can't put up with snakes.

I thought instantly of the princess in the fairytale, but I want my happy ending.

Which means that I won't wait for a prince to save me.

Because I might be waiting a long time.

I can't even get a dog to wake up.

I'm going to find an exterminator.

And I'll live happily ever after.

Moist

BY LISA

You have heard the myth of Sisyphus, the Greek king who was required to roll a massive boulder up a mountain, and when it reached the top, it would roll down to the bottom, so he had to start all over again, an endless exercise in futility.

So obviously we're talking about moisturizing your legs.

Don't ask me when I started moisturizing my legs, but it was back when I actually cared.

I would shave my legs and moisturize them, because that was something you were supposed to do.

We're talking my twenties, thirties, and forties, and I used a variety of leg moisturizers. Those were the years I was married and divorced and married and divorced, so there was probably some correlation, the common denominator being that a man was seeing my legs, even if it was a man I loved and/or hated.

In any event, I got very happily single, and while I was dating, I kept my legs as smooth as a Barbie doll. I was looking for Ken, and though I didn't find him, I found an array of better things to do with my time. But I have to admit, my personal grooming fell down, limbwise.

I didn't always shave my legs, especially in winter, when I was not only celibate, but freezing.

Still, I moisturized my legs every day, on girl autopilot.

But then in my fifties, I stopped doing even that, even on special occasions, like if I had a book signing.

God bless pants.

And today's the day that I might stop moisturizing my legs.

I'm looking at them with new eyes. And I'm thinking of Sisyphus.

Because the bottom line is that I'm fifty-nine years old and I've been moisturizing my legs for as long as I can remember, and it doesn't seem to be working. Don't tell me the difference is the product. In my student days, I used drugstore products, and then, when I made more money, I started buying moisturizers in the department store, thinking they would be better.

They weren't.

The only difference was that department-store moisturizing creams were called crèmes, so they may have worked for the French, but not for me.

I wised up and went back to the drugstore, where I bought a big white tub of good old Cetaphil, which is not coincidentally shaped like a rolling boulder.

They should call it Cetaphus.

Because the bottom line is, what purpose is all this moisturizing serving?

If you have to moisturize your legs every day, what is getting moisturized?

And why isn't it staying that way?

And if it isn't staying moisturized, which it obviously isn't, then why bother?

It puts me in mind of some advice Martha Stewart gave somewhere, with respect to basting a turkey. Her cooking tip was that basting a turkey has no effect whatsoever. She said the moistness of the meat depended completely on how the turkey was raised and fed, then whether it was overcooked or not.

So you see the analogy.

Turkeys aren't moisturized by basting.

Women aren't either.

Maybe it lasts for a day, but that's not long enough for me.

That's why I don't make my bed anymore.

So if I've stopped making my bed, I should stop moisturizing my legs.

I've only been feeling this more strongly as I've gotten older and my skin has changed so much.

And it's not just that they've gone from dry to Sahara.

The other day, I looked down at my legs and didn't recognize them as mine.

Or as even human.

They were positively scaly.

There are fish with better legs.

Oh, wait.

Okay, dragons.

Not only that, but they're insanely ashy.

The Bible says we came from dust and to dust we shall return.

But so soon?

Still, there's truth in the wisdom of the ancients.

I don't mean me.

I mean the Bible and the Greek myths.

You can't beat Father Time with a tub of grease.

OK FREUD

BY FRANCESCA

I feel like I'm the last of my friends to try two things: online dating and therapy.

I think I need both.

Or more specifically, I think I need one for the other.

I'm just not sure in which order.

There are times in everyone's life when you have a tough season. Mine was this winter, when I ended things with my long-term boyfriend and my grandmother passed away, within the span of a month. I knew why I was sad about my grandmother, that part was easy to understand. But within my sadness over the breakup, there was something else — fear.

As in, that was a close one.

I'm entering the Era of Big Decisions when it comes to love and life partners. What if I'm choosing the wrong partners for my needs and hopes?

All of my exes have been great people, just

ultimately not great for me. But I'm at an age where my next unsuitable boyfriend could easily become my unsuitable husband.

Or my first ex-husband.

And I want to nip that in the bud. Whatever I have within me, genetic or emotional, that could sow the seeds of a divorce, I want to pull out by the roots, now.

Basically, I want couple's therapy before I'm in a couple.

One thing I'd want to fix in therapy is I want to dump dudes faster. Some people need help keeping a relationship together, I need help busting them apart.

This is why it's such a misconception that children of divorce don't respect marriage as much as children from "intact" families. If anything, I've overcompensated. In a relationship, I'm a fixer, a helper. I expect to struggle and sacrifice more than I expect to have fun and be happy. I'm not a doormat, but I can be too forgiving for my own good.

I need that inner referee to shout YERRR-ROUTT! after three strikes.

Instead of thirteen.

And in general, I feel like I could use an emotional tune-up, a fifty-thousand-mile checkup before the age-ometer clicks to thirty.

So my quest to be and to find a good partner has led me to my next question:

How do you find a good therapist?

Sure, I could ask my GP for a referral, but this is an important relationship. I don't just need a phone number and a PhD.

I need a match.

I'll be entrusting this person with my most intimate, vulnerable thoughts. And part of the bargain is I'd be privileging their opinion above my own. I'm entrusting them with my emotional health.

What if my therapist has daddy issues?

That would be the blind leading the blind.

I've heard horror stories of bad therapists. Therapists who over-prescribe medication, therapists who only want to burn incense and analyze dreams, therapists who drive wedges where they're supposed to build bridges.

Friends tell me I should meet with a therapist and see how I like him or her, and that I'll know if it's a good fit or not.

But if I knew who was a good fit for me, I wouldn't need therapy.

Because I recognize the ways my personality could make this evaluation process hard. One, I have too much respect for authority. I'm a Goody-two-shoes, a teacher's pet, or, what they call in therapy-speak: a people-pleaser.

See, I already learned the lingo. In case there's a pop quiz.

So it would be hard for me to trust my own opinion of a psychologist over a psychologist's. That framed Latinate degree would look down on me from the wall, saying "whose name is on here, hmm?" They're the experts.

I just have to remember that I'm the foremost expert on Francesca Serritella. My life's work is in the field.

I can also see the ways in which I could be downright obstructionist to good therapy. I think upon first meeting, I'd be hell-bent on showing him or her how sane I am, how well adjusted, how insightful.

I'd do anything to convince my shrink I don't need a shrink.

I'd try to be one step ahead of them. Already, when discussing relationships with my friends, I'm always prefacing my feelings:

"I know this is the codependent in me speaking . . ."

"I know I probably get this from my dad, but . . ."

"I know . . ." "I know . . ." "I know, but . . ."

But I don't know.

I'm just not sure I can admit that to a complete stranger yet.

Other than you, that is.

And if I did have some doubts about a psychologist I was seeing, how do I know when to jump ship? How much discomfort during therapy is part of the path to personal growth, versus just a dud therapist?

What if there's not a better one out there? What if the next one is worse?

See this is already sounding like my problem with dating.

In both cases, I'm afraid of making myself vulnerable to the wrong person.

So I need OK Cupid for therapists.

OK Freud.

SWEET TOOTH

BY LISA

Good news for people who live in the Philadelphia area.

We're one of the top thirty cities with the largest number of Sugar Daddies.

Yay!

I discovered this news item recently, after in-depth investigative journalism.

In other words, somebody sent me a press release.

This would be inside information into the workings of the modern-day newspaper business, by the way. The number of journalists is shrinking, so PR companies routinely send press releases to suggest news stories to the hardy few that remain.

And to me, too.

I don't consider myself a real journalist.

I'm comic relief to the real journalists.

Nevertheless, I receive probably one hundred emails per day addressed to me as a Women's Interests Reporter.

Because somebody thinks Women's Interests are different from Men's Interests.

To be fair, they might be right, but that's a column for another day.

I am a complete expert on Women's Interests, but if I knew what Men were Interested in, I wouldn't be Divorced Twice.

So to stay on point, most of the press releases are glorified ads for new beauty products, hair gels, makeups, and the like, but today I received a press release advertising a dating website that was established for Sugar Daddies who want to meet Sugar Babies, to experience the Sugar Lifestyle.

First, let's define some terms.

A Sugar Daddy isn't that candy you remember, which was caramel taffy on a stick, guaranteed to take out a filling.

According to the website, a Sugar Daddy is a man who is about forty-four years old, with a net worth of around $7 million.

It doesn't matter if he is a nice person, what he looks like, or what he thinks is important in life.

He has $7 million in the piggybank, which is an acceptable substitute for everything else.

Except maybe an actual piggy.

Sugar Babies aren't those chewy caramel taffy candies that you remember, either.

According to the website, Sugar Babies are "attractive people looking for the finer things in life." They "appreciate exotic trips," "a luxurious lifestyle," and "wealthy people."

The website doesn't specify the age of your basic Sugar Baby.

I'm guessing she's out of the stroller, but not by much.

Come to think of it, I'm not sure I believe that your basic Sugar Daddy is only forty-four years old.

That would be your basic Sugar Son.

Probably the ideal Sugar Couple would be a woman in a stroller and a man in a wheelchair.

To sign up for the website as a Sugar Daddy, you have to agree to "pamper Sugar Babies in return for companionship."

If you are signing up as a Sugar Baby, you agree to "provide companionship in exchange for being pampered."

In other words, prostitution.

Or maybe just pampering.

Or pandering.

The website suggests that you could also sign up as a Sugar Momma, but I would bet my last million bucks that there are very few Sugar Mommas.

I say this as an expert in Women's

Interests.

My bet is that most women are like me, and if I had $7 million, I wouldn't be interested in pampering anybody but me.

My Pampers days are over.

Come to think of it, that sums it up completely.

Most women have spent their entire lives taking care of husbands, kids, dogs, then the dogs of their kids.

And in my case, the kids of their dogs.

And by the time they reach the ancient age of forty-four, which is evidently their dotage in Sugar Years, the last thing in the world that most women want to do is to keep taking care of everything in sight.

The website also defines the "Sugar Lifestyle," in which "users are on the same page," don't have to "read between the lines," and "know what they want."

I thought it would be simpler, being called the Sugar Lifestyle.

I myself already live the Sugar Lifestyle, and it involves . . . Sugar.

The small print says that relationships are easier when "goals and starting points are already set forth before entering said relationship."

How romantic.

I went to law school, which was sexier.

According to the press release, there are 2.95 Sugar Daddies per one thousand males who live in Philadelphia.

I'm kind of wondering about the leftover .05.

I seem to recall dating him.

You're Just Some Appliance That I Used to Know

BY LISA

There are joys to empty nesting, and they increase as the nest gets emptier.

I just realized this the other day, when I was walking through my kitchen and there was a large object on my right that I barely recognized.

My oven.

It's big and boxy and has four burners in the top, and I remember standing around it, doing something called cooking.

But that might be a thing of the past.

Because right now, I can't remember the last time I cooked.

I looked at the oven and wondered if I could yank it out and replace it with a TV.

Or better yet, another refrigerator.

In other words, an appliance I really love, instead of one that I used to love.

I think I broke up with my oven.

It might have become my ex-oven.

In fact, we have found Thing Three.

It wasn't always thus.

When Daughter Francesca was growing up, I used to love my oven very deeply and I really did enjoy cooking.

I'm not Mother Mary's daughter for nothing.

Cooking is part of my DNA. The Flying Scottolines have tomato sauce in our veins.

And in the early years after Daughter Francesca flew the coop, I had fun cooking hot meals for myself, at least twice a day. I made a goat cheese and spinach omelet for breakfast, a nice arugula salad for lunch, and I always cooked fish, veggies, rice, or whatever for dinner, even though it was just me.

I made a point of this, for my own psyche.

I was proving to myself that I still mattered even though I lived alone, which was completely true, and I believed that somehow the trouble I went to for myself was proof of my self-worth.

What a bunch of crap.

I'm at the next stage of life, which is when you stop proving dumb stuff to yourself.

You stop proving stuff altogether.

You officially have Nothing to Prove.

You don't do anything unless you want to.

You decide exactly how and when to spend your time.

You stop doing things out of obligation, even to yourself.

You realize that salmon is not related to self-worth.

I think this is called maturity, and I wish it hadn't taken me fifty-nine years to attain.

Better late than never.

Anyway, it's not like I made a conscious decision to stop cooking, but all of a sudden I started thinking that salad would make a good dinner, or yogurt and honey, or a cheese sandwich.

Now the way I see it is, I have so much self-worth that I should not put myself to the trouble of cooking for myself. It's a strange thing, considering that cooking was so much a part of my life, but on the other hand, I have more free time at night to read, work, or watch TV — mainly, the Food Network.

Now that I've stopped cooking, I watch more cooking shows than ever.

Watching other people cook is the new cooking.

But I watch the cooking shows differently than I used to. I don't try to remember the ingredients they're using or the things they're doing, because I have no intention of ever making the recipes.

I'm not taking the course for a grade

anymore.

On the contrary, I'm barely auditing.

Yay!

The only downside to my new life is that once you decide that you don't have to cook a proper dinner, then all bets are off.

If there's a slippery slope, I'm sliding to the bottom.

Last week for various dinners I had Fiber One cereal, Honeycrisp apples, roasted red peppers, leftover Stacy's Pita chips with cheese, and a massive bag of popcorn. Dessert was Hershey's Kisses with Almonds and gummi vitamins.

Yum!

But not exactly healthy eating.

Hmmm.

Somebody needs a mother.

But I've flown my own coop.

WOMEN'S RIGHTS AND WRONGS

BY LISA

Everywhere you look you can see enormous regard for women, especially among big business.

I'm talking about two great new products.

The first is the wine rack.

No, not that wine rack.

Not that shelf with the holes that hold wine bottles.

Silly.

I'm talking about a bra that has two plastic bags, one in each cup, and you can fill the bags with wine, which you can drink through a tube attached to the bra.

The "wine rack."

Get it?

It's so punny!

Anyway, what a clever idea, right?

I'm sure that every woman has wondered whether she could drink wine out of her bra.

That is, everyone but me.

Although to be fair, I have wondered if I could eat chocolate cake out of my bra.

Then I could have cup cakes!

See, I can think of stupid puns, too!

By the way, I don't know where your breasts go if the cups of your bra are occupied by wine bags. Evidently, you can't be picky when your underwear doubles as a beverage-delivery system.

And who doesn't want their wine warmed by body heat?

In any event, it's good to know that American business is constantly thinking of innovative ways to meet the needs of women.

Alcoholic women.

In fact, if you look up the wine rack online, they call it "every girl's best friend."

Really?

More like every girl's best frenemy.

Because, let's be real. It's a bra.

Every girl's best friend is going braless.

Amazingly, in addition to the wine rack, I came across another genius product for women, called the Shewee.

Yes, you read that right.

According to its website, the Shewee is a "urinating device that allows women to urinate when they're on the go."

In other words, if you have to go while

you're on the go.

I'd like to describe a Shewee to you, but good taste prevails.

For a change.

The bottom line is that it's plastic and it's shaped like — well, it's for girls who have penis envy.

In other words, no girl ever.

Only a man would come up with the idea that women have penis envy. Because anybody who has ever seen a penis knows that no woman would want one.

You know what's in men's pants that we want?

A wallet.

To stay on point, the Shewee is the "the original female urination device."

Copycats, beware.

Accept no substitutions.

Like a Tupperware funnel.

The website says that the Shewee is perfect for "camping, festivals, cycling, during pregnancy, long car journeys, climbing, sailing, skiing, the list is endless!"

It doesn't say anything about being middle-aged.

Too bad, because I'm pretty sure that if you're middle-aged, you'll want one of these babies. Even if you don't camp or go to festivals, and your days of pregnancy are behind you.

We know why, don't we, ladies?

Do I have to spell it out for you — in the snow?

I myself am about to order a gross.

Because it's gross.

My favorite thing about the Shewee is that it comes in seven different colors.

Oddly, there was no yellow.

If you ask me, that's a no-brainer.

Get your marketing together, people.

My favorite color was "Power Pink."

Because nothing says empowered like being able to pee where you want, damn it.

Sayonara, rest stops.

I'm gonna pee in my car!

Woot woot!

So with the holidays around the corner, now you know the perfect gifts for all your girlfriends.

If you get them the wine rack, I guarantee they're going to need the Shewee.

HOT OR NOT AT THE GYM
BY FRANCESCA

Getting started is the hardest part of any growing experience.

I can tell you it gets better, because I'm on the other side of it now. But in the beginning of any fitness journey, you're going to feel bad about yourself. Even when you're working out at the gym, you'll feel bad. Especially when you're working out at the gym. It's a cruel trick.

Because when you feel bad about how you look, everyone else looks great. I never notice more thin people than on those days that I feel fat.

This is the definition of neuroses.

But it's amplified at the gym.

Those first months working out at my new gym were brutal.

Naturally, I was convinced it was the gym's fault.

It's in downtown Manhattan, home to fashion models and gay men — the two most beautiful demographics statistically.

I'd pass the mats and always see some lovely, lithe woman stretching out her spider limbs. Or some gorgeous man making squat sets look like B-roll from *Magic Mike.*

Maybe I just tell myself the men are gay because I can't have them.

But these people were just too fit to comfortably exercise with.

In other words, this gym was too effective.

Everyone there seemed so purposeful except me. I felt conspicuously clueless wandering around the machines, so my solution was to take a lot of group classes instead. But that plan wasn't without its drawbacks.

See, I work best with positive reinforcement, and the mirror was being kind of a jerk.

During Barre Burn, for instance, I'd see myself in the mirror and feel like Santa in line with the Rockettes.

The other girls' tank tops pulled only across their breasts like comic-book heroines, while my tummy pushed at my shirt.

My jumping jacks were more jumping jiggles.

And thank God I got to face away from the mirror for downward dog.

I didn't even have the right clothes. There was a uniform among the women of trim black yoga pants and cute strappy sport tops. I typically wore an oversize T-shirt and puffy basketball shorts.

My mental spin on this was that I'm simply too down-to-earth to buy nice clothes to sweat in. But after a couple weeks of avoiding my own reflection, it occurred to me:

They're not showing off; I'm hiding.

So I bought some new, flattering tank tops, slimming pants of my own, and a sports bra that showed tasteful, workout-cleave instead of binding my breasts into the dreaded mono-boob.

And I felt a little better about myself.

Money *can* buy you self-love.

But the locker room was a fresh hell. Who are these women who wear such beautiful underwear to the gym? Matching sets, lace, *thongs.*

Squats in a thong? Ouch.

Lunges? (Shudder)

I saw one woman in such elaborate lingerie, I can only assume it was Dita Von Teese without makeup.

Personally, I work out in drugstore granny-panties, and I don't apologize for it.

I just need a pair that say, "My Other

Underwear Is a G-String."

And there's always that one show-off in the women's locker room. Like the woman who blow-dries her hair in the mirror while standing stark naked. Or the one who lathers her body in moisturizer with more sensuality than Cinemax after midnight.

Your nipples aren't that chapped, dear.

But the steam room is my oasis.

It's the antidote of the see-and-be-seen nature of the rest of the gym. There's a collective understanding that if we're all going to be naked in a little room together and have any hope of relaxing, we must suspend our judgmental and self-critical impulses and allow ourselves to just breathe.

Bodies of all ages, shapes, and sizes are equal in the foggy eyes of the steam room.

I give myself all sorts of mental pep talks in there. I work out plot twists in the novel I'm ever editing. I envision meetings with agents going well. I say positive affirmations about what I like about my body. I plan out date outfits whether or not I have a date. And I always leave feeling detoxified.

Which is why I dislike this one young woman. She always struts in the steam room completely naked, not even the gesture of carrying a towel to lie down on.

That's just unsanitary.

Now, is she beautiful? Absolutely. She looks in her early twenties, blond, and in perfect shape. She's stunning and she knows it. Am I jealous? You bet. But I swear this isn't sour grapes. I'm not taking issue with her beauty. I'm taking issue with the performance.

This is her routine. First, she makes a big show of standing and posing as she rakes her fingers through her hair before twisting it up.

Please, now you're making it unsanitary for us and getting your hairs everywhere. And I speak as a curly-haired shedder myself when I say, keep it outside.

Then she begins to stretch. We're talking full-on-naked lunges.

The general etiquette in the steam room is a benign disregard between women. So when The Hot Girl started her naked yoga near where I was lying down, I resisted the urge to move away so that I wouldn't offend her. But as she did a full bend right by my head, I wished for more steam to cover my eyes.

I saw more of her than I've seen of myself.

And let it be noted that she doesn't do the awkward stretches. You know the ones, where your belly folds, or your one hand behind your back blindly gropes for the other hand. No, she only does the sexy stretches — those combinations of sun salutations and Playmate poses.

My point is, it kills the vibe. You can feel the collective shift of the other women to cover themselves when she enters.

But then the other day, I entered the steam room while The Hot Girl was in the midst of her act, and the other women were tucked away in the corners, avoiding her. I hoped the steam hid my side-eye as I took a seat as far away from her vagina as possible.

And then, while she was arching her back in some sort of breast stretch, it happened.

She farted.

Twice.

Once mid-stretch, and again when she tried to sit down like nothing happened.

And we all heard it.

Farting in a steam room is pretty rude. It's one step above space suit for impolite places to bust a toot.

But luckily it didn't smell. Because, of course, it didn't.

For about thirty seconds, The Hot Girl tried to act casual, but then the embarrassment got to her and she high-tailed, or likely clench-tailed, it out of there.

A couple of us giggled after she left.

Not to laugh at her, per se.

But because no human can escape the occasional indignity of the gym.

TWISTED SISTER

BY LISA

So it turns out I have an occupational hazard.

I'm not complaining, because at least I have an occupation.

The only problem with my occupation is that I spend a lot of time occupying a chair.

And the first occupational hazard is that my butt is spreading.

What, I can't blame that on my job?

Fair enough.

Thanks a lot, carbohydrates.

Actually, the best part of my job is that I get to sit around all day in a chair, and I have set up my office so that my desk is in the middle of the room, with the TV to the left. I keep the TV on while I'm working, just to have some background noise that isn't dogs farting.

But a year ago, my back started to hurt. I ignored it for a while, then when my book deadline was finally finished, I got my big butt to the doctor, who said:

"We X-rayed your back, and you have scoliosis."

I thought he was mispronouncing my last name, which everybody does, and I don't blame them. I tell them Scottoline rhymes with fettuccine, but this word sounded different. Lisa Scoliosis isn't a good name. I asked, "Scolli-what-is?"

The doctor answered, "It means a rotation of the spinal column, but in your case it's not congenital. So you're an author?"

"Yes," I told him. I always put that on my medical records, so that my doctors will buy my books. I would say it's free advertising, but given the general cost of a doctor's visit, they would have to buy 3,293,737 of my books for me to break even.

The doctor continued, "So you probably spend a lot of time sitting and you must be turning to the left. Why are you turning to the left?"

"Because that's where the TV is?"

"Hmmm," he said, just like a doctor in the movies.

Or on TV.

I was getting the general drift, because I'm a mystery writer and I don't need a lot of clues. "So you mean to tell me that just because I sat on my butt and watched TV while I worked, for twenty-five years, I rotated my spine?"

"Yes."

So this was all TV's fault. Thank God it wasn't my fault. It can never be my fault.

The doctor added, "And you're probably crossing your legs, too."

I thought about it. "I probably am. How else can you keep a dog on your lap while you work?"

The doctor laughed. He thought I was kidding.

You and I know I wasn't.

Maybe he should start reading my books.

Anyway, I got serious. "Now what do we do?"

"Work out."

I tried not to groan.

Why is "working out" always the answer?

Why is the answer never "chocolate cake"?

Meanwhile, I tell the doctor that I walk the dogs, ride a bike, and even sit like a lump on the back of a pony, but he says none of this counts. He sends me to physical therapy, telling me to dress comfortably.

I don't need to be told to dress comfortably.

I'm a middle-aged woman.

We're too smart to dress any other way.

I've already gone to two sessions of physical therapy, which are held in a big open gym with a lot of other people who were sent there for respectable reasons that had nothing to do with watching too much television.

There, I do twenty reps of the Backward Bend, the Press-Up, Bridging, and an array of other horrible exercises, all of which require a Neutral Spine.

This doesn't come easily to me.

Not only because I hate working out, but because I'm not neutral about anything.

I have opinions.

My least favorite of the exercises is one called Isometric Stabilization, and the directions on the sheet say that I'm supposed to "tighten abdominal muscles as if tightening a belt."

In other words, suck it in.

Oddly, I've been doing this exercise my entire life.

In any photo of me, I'm engaging in Isometric Stabilization.

Now I have a sheet of floor exercises to do three times day at home, with pictures to show me the correct form.

Oddly, none of the pictures shows my dogs jumping on my head, licking my face, or walking across my chest while I do the exercises.

Any pet owner who tries to work out at home knows how helpful dogs can be.

If you have twenty reps to do, good luck getting through rep two.

Or maybe they are helpful?

GOOD GRIEF

BY LISA

Today is Mother Mary's birthday, which is both a sad and happy occasion, since she passed away in April.

Good grief.

It's an interesting expression and applies perfectly, capturing completely the push and pull of emotions of a day like this, on which I'm mentally celebrating her life and mourning her passing.

In fact, it's the paradox of death itself, which is losing somebody and loving them, both at the same time.

We don't stop loving somebody just because they're not around anymore.

And that's true whether they're in the next room, on a trip to Belize, or simply passed into another realm.

They're away, but they're here, both at once.

Time and space are conflated on a day like this, collapsed into one another, each crashing the other's party.

At least that's how I've been feeling, these seven months past her passing — which never really passes.

I'm not sure if this is the correct way to experience the death of a parent, but it's the only one I've got, and it's the same one I had ten years ago, when my father passed away.

To me, they're both still here, and this is either sound mental health or the most merciful form of denial.

In any event, I'll take it.

I have no choice.

And to be completely honest, it isn't the way I thought it would be. I spent most of my life fearing the loss of my parents, because I was close to them both, but in different ways.

My father was fun-loving, smart, and warm, a benign presence in my life. He lived nearby and he was my go-to guy for advice, a sure laugh, or an outing to a movie. Father Frank would go anywhere, at any time. He was game and supremely easy to get along with. As a novelist, I know that actions describe character better than words, and the act that describes him perfectly is his habit of going to the movies on a Saturday night, around eight o'clock and buying a ticket for whichever movie he could see the most of at the time.

When he went to the movies, he went to the movies.

All of them, any one.

He never planned it, because it wasn't his nature. He figured all the movies were pretty good, and he never met a movie or a person that he didn't like.

Mother Mary, whom you know if you've read about her, was his exact opposite, which was probably why they were headed for divorce the day they married.

Another interesting conflation of time and space.

Another paradox.

Mother Mary was feisty, strong, and always ready to crack wise. She was a survivor of an impoverished childhood, the youngest of nineteen children. I won't repeat the many stories about her herein, but because her personality was so much larger than her four-foot-eleven frame and her influence so pervasive, I would've expected her passing to leave a massive hole in my life, like a vacuum in space into which things disappeared, a void like a bottomless loss.

But that hasn't happened at all.

Which is good for me and probably for

the universe as a whole, because it sounded so scary.

I'm experiencing the loss of her, but the way I experienced the loss of my father. I'm not stricken, like a blow that leaves me reeling with the force of its impact, but it's more like a fact of life — that runs alongside the fact of death.

She's with me all the time even though she isn't.

I don't talk to her in my head, like other people do, but I hear her voice in my head and I know what she would say in any given situation.

Probably, so do you.

And if you have your mother plus Mother Mary in your head, I wish you luck.

People always joke that daughters become their mothers, and in my case, become their fathers too, and I think all of us embody the best of our parents.

And if we're trying to live our lives the best way possible, we're keeping what we loved about them and deleting the rest, like when a sure-handed editor goes over the first draft of the manuscript. The edited story morphs and changes, but the first draft — our mothers and our fathers — remain in the story, present behind the sentences themselves, and that essence abides always, never really going away.

And so we are, each of us, a book.

But no one of us is truly finished. We're constantly rewriting ourselves, and the possibilities are limitless. We never know where our own narrative will lead, or which plot twist will come out which way.

It's not The End.

We're not in final draft, not while we draw breath.

So breathe in.

And keep writing.

CARBS OF PEACE

BY FRANCESCA

It's commonly held wisdom that one healthy choice leads to another. So it seemed fitting that I discovered a health food store on the way home from my new gym.

The store is called Health & Harmony, and as soon as I passed through its doors, I knew I had entered the rabbit hole of rabbit food.

Rows upon rows of products I'd never seen before in brightly colored packaging with words I'd never read.

Chia, and kombucha, and flax, oh my!

I was dazzled. I've always been an adventurous eater, but since I started my new and improved diet in the spring, the result has been a rather repetitive rotation of lean meals.

This was like Willy Wonka's factory with no high-fructose corn syrup.

When I call this a health food store, I don't mean a box of Kashi cereal. Kashi is for amateurs. This was some next-level, Goop.com kind of stuff.

The dairy aisle, for example, isn't hemmed in by the confines of a cow. There's almond milk, coconut milk, soy milk, Tofutti cream cheese, anything *but* milk from a mammal.

Think outside the teat.

And forget that Greek yogurt that John Stamos sells. Health & Harmony is immune to Uncle Jesse's charms. Here, they sell Siggi's Icelandic-style Skyr.

Don't be scared, or skyrred. Skyr is just Icelandic for yogurt.

And it's delicious. They have the most unusual flavors, like Coconut, Orange & Ginger, and Pumpkin Spice, so of course I had to try them all.

Gluten is enemy number one at this store. Every pretzel, cracker, and cookie says GLUTEN FREE across the front. Even things that obviously wouldn't have gluten, like cheese, peanut butter, or edamame, proudly display their gluten prejudice.

But what if I want gluten? Or not so much that I want it, but I'm afraid of what they're substituting it with.

Remember when we all hopped on the nonfat bandwagon before we realized that meant replacing fat with enough sugar to send you into glycemic shock?

Or when we fell for sugar-free without realizing that meant carcinogenic-aspartame-full?

Better the devil you know . . .

So I stick with the unusual but still pure foods. Most of the time. I confess, I was intrigued by a bag of white noodles floating in water called Shirataki noodles. They look like spaghetti, but they are mysteriously calorie-free.

My foggy memory of chemistry class says that a calorie is a unit of heat energy, so if this food has no calories, does that mean you can't kill it with fire?

It is the devil's noodle.

But carb-free pasta, are you kidding? Mephistopheles, where do I sign?

(Holy sh-t, guys, I just Wikipedia'd Shirataki noodles, because I am a serious author who does serious research, and it, for real, said that another name is "Devil's Tongue Noodles." I was just joking before! Now I'm scared.)

Also, it seems every food at this store has live active cultures in it. Apparently, bacteria in your food is a good thing.

I knew the five-second rule was real.

For instance, there's an entire section of sauerkrauts, because pickled is *in* this season. On a whim, I plucked the Spicy

The Devil's Noodle

Wakame Ginger Kimchi off the shelf. The back of the bag had a list of rhetorical questions:

"Do you know that raw, fermented foods are alive?"

No, I thought I was eating vegetarian.

"Fresh kraut is full of living, healthful micro-organisms that need room to grow."

Do I need to save for their college?

"The nifty valve at the top of this pouch allows the Kraut to breathe."

Concerning.

But I bought the wacky ginger kimchi anyway, and you know what? Those living, breathing organisms taste great with mayon-naise!

Well, a store clerk convinced me to switch to Vegenaise (diary-free, egg-free, GLUTEN-free), but it tastes the same, almost.

When I cracked down on my diet, I pretty much eliminated all my favorite snacks. I was rarely consuming them for nutritional value and mostly eating them to solve problems such as: "I'm bored," "I have to work to earn money," "This isn't that good an episode," and "Why isn't he texting me back?"

But Health & Harmony sells all manner of guilt-free snacks. My favorite are the Cassava Root Chips. They look like potato chips, but they're made of a tough, fibrous root.

And if I don't already have you at "tough, fibrous root," they also have 40 percent less fat than a regular potato chip.

I had never heard of cassava, but I read on the back, "The Cassava tree grows all over Asia, South America, and Africa. Cassava root is the primary energy source for 800 million people all over the planet!"

I paused to consider that 800 million people are forced to have a diet primarily fueled by a tree root. And I don't think they do it to watch their figure.

But, if you don't mind the side of privilege-awareness, this is a great snack.

And the bag said the chips are Certified Rain Forest Alliance. So at least I wasn't ripping cassava root out of the hands of indigenous peoples.

Speaking of certifications, all the store's products appear very well educated. I realized this with the only snack I tried and hated, the Kale + Chia Chips. I generally love kale, and I don't really understand what chia is, but combined, they tasted like tortilla chips made of peat moss. However, I couldn't knock its pedigree:

Certified Kosher, Certified Gluten Free, Certified Vegan, and Certified MSG and Trans-fat Free.

The chips have more meaningless degrees than James Franco.

But perhaps my favorite food discovered at Health & Harmony is Peace Cereal, specifically in the Baobab Coconut flavor.

What is a baobab, you ask? I'd only previously encountered the word in *The Little Prince,* but I remember when studying that book in French class, the baobab trees are a) parasitic "bad seeds" that will destroy planets with their roots, and b) possibly an allegory for the Nazis.

But they also taste amazing with coconut!

What do they taste like? Between you and me, I would say the flakes taste like a Joy sugar cone.

But don't tell the clerk I said so.

All I know for sure is that I can go through a box a week.

Before, I had completely cut out cereals because I thought they had too much sugar, but this is a cereal I can feel good about! It says right on the box:

"A contribution will be made to non-profit causes for every Peace cereal product sold."

Eager to justify eating fistfuls of cereal in front of a *Say Yes to the Dress* marathon, I went to the website for more details.

I think I was the first person to do so, since the charities on their site haven't been updated since 2012. But they support national parks, breast and ovarian cancer research, and a New Hampshire animal rescue devoted to disabled animals.

Do you want to tell Misty, the one-eyed, arthritic Labrador, that you can't help her find her food bowl, because you're cutting carbs?

I didn't either.

So every time I came home from the gym, I'd stop at Health & Harmony and pick up new, unusual foods to try, feeling like a pirate sailing home with exotic treasure.

But you know what happened? All that booty went right to my ass.

I realized my health food store is making me fat.

That's what happens if you sell your soul for a diet.

THRU FLU

BY LISA

I can't always tell the truth from the bull.

And this is nowhere more apparent than when it comes to flu shots.

Also my marital history, but that's a subject for another day.

I don't know whether to get a flu shot, and for some reason, flu shots are having a moment.

I say this because I went to the doctor to see about my ear infection, and before the receptionist even checked me in, she asked, "Do you want a flu shot?"

"Um, I don't think so," I answered, surprised. "Should I get one?"

"We recommend it. I can have the nurse give you one right now, while you wait to see the doctor."

I hesitated. "Well, I have a fever, so maybe this isn't the best time for a flu shot."

"I'm sure it's fine."

I wasn't so sure. "Maybe I'll ask the doctor and see what he thinks."

"Okay." The receptionist shrugged.

I admit, I was just using the fever thing for an excuse. Because I know this isn't scientific, but something about a vaccine scares me.

Let me repeat. I know this is completely unscientific.

Don't write me an angry email, and please, for God's sake, don't take any medical advice from me.

I'm just speaking for the great unwashed when I say it seems counterintuitive to me that in order to protect me from something I might not get, you have to give it to me for sure.

I know, as an intellectual matter, that I didn't get smallpox because I was given a vaccination God-knows-when, and also that I didn't have polio because they gave us the vaccine in a sugar cube.

Back then, I was a kid and I couldn't say no — to things that were good for me.

But now I'm making up for lost time.

Please note that nobody at the doctor's office asked me if I wanted my flu shot in a sugar cube.

Or in you-know-what.

(Chocolate cake.)

They might have gotten a different answer.

You can catch more flies with honey than you can with needles.

And I guess my other issue, also completely irrational, is that I don't want to live my life being afraid of all the bad things that can happen and protecting myself against them.

If I get the flu, I'll get the flu.

I'll feel crappy for a while, then it will go away.

In any event, I've never had a flu shot.

And I haven't had the flu, in recent memory.

For me, flu shots have gone into the category of insurance, which is something that I pay for to ward off some horrible thing that will happen, except that when the horrible thing happens, I end up paying for it anyway.

In fact, this happened to me just last week, when they told me at my physical therapist's office that my deductible was so high, it would be cheaper for me to pay for the physical therapy sessions out of pocket instead of going through my health insurance.

So now I have become my car, and when I crash, I'm paying my own way.

At the same time that I'm paying my car insurer.

And my heath insurer.

Anyway, what happened when I saw the doctor was that we got so engrossed talking about the ear infection that I forgot to ask him about whether I should get a flu shot, so when I went to the desk to check out, it was the cashier's turn to ask me: "Before you leave, would you like a flu shot?"

But I still wasn't sure. "I forgot to ask the doctor, so let's forget it."

The cashier blinked. "But we recommend it. I can have the nurse do it."

"Thank you, but no." I reached in my wallet for my co-pay, which is when I began to wonder if it wasn't the flu shot that was having a moment, but me.

Many moments, in fact.

Because I was probably at that age where medical professionals start asking you if you need a flu shot.

But they're too tactful to say, "Hey old lady, shouldn't you be thinking about your mortality? One flu and you could fly away, if you get my drift."

Message received.

And this old lady reserves the right to be contrary.

No flu shot.

Until good sense prevails.

TREAD LIGHTLY

BY LISA

I'm about to make the smartest purchase of my life, or the dumbest.

Before I tell you what it is, let me tell you why I'm doing it, because that's even dumber, or smarter, depending on how the story ends.

I first saw one of these contraptions last year, when I happened to be doing research online.

Okay, I admit, I was wasting time online.

Which might be redundant.

Yesterday, I happened to be wasting time online again and I kept noticing sidebar ads popping up, which as we all know now, are based on the things tracking our online behavior. They call the things that do this cookies, but if you ask me, it's the one kind of cookie I don't like.

In other words, chocolate chips taste better than computer chips.

Anyway, the cookies in your computer

send you ads about the products you've looked at in the past, and if you're like me, you forget you've been looking at these products, so when the ads pop up and offer you these products, you get the eerie sensation that your computer is reading your mind.

When it's just that your computer has a better memory than you do.

To come to my point, a long time ago, I was kind of curious about treadmill desks, because it seemed like such a crazy thing to me. If you don't know what a treadmill desk is, it's a special treadmill that only goes two to four miles an hour, or walking at a slow pace, and it's outfitted with a desktop that is eyeball height, so that you can work on your computer at the same time that you're standing up and walking on the treadmill.

Ridiculous, right?

I thought it was, too.

So ridiculous, in fact, that I was actually going to write about how ridiculous it was that people have to be working so hard and multitasking like crazy, so that they can't even take time from work to take a walk, for God's sake.

And of course the very notion of working while on a treadmill is too good a metaphor for a writer to pass up.

The only thing better would be a rat in a race.

The rat race, get it?

Does anybody still even know that expression?

Okay, so to get back to the story, there I was online and all of these ads kept popping up for treadmill desks, and since then I've started having back problems from sitting so much for work. In fact, the physical therapist told me my back would benefit if I switched to a standing desk.

I need a desk for my discs!

But I'm never one to leave well enough alone.

Why get a standing desk when you can have a walking desk?

I mean, why should your desk just get to sit there, doing nothing?

So I clicked on the ad for the treadmill desk.

And I started reading.

All of a sudden, it started not to seem so ridiculous anymore.

In fact, the company that makes the desks says that it makes fitness-at-work products that "target the 55+ health-conscious consumer."

I instantly thought, ME!

So I spent some time on the website,

watching the sales video of the people happily typing away on their computers while they were walking on treadmills.

And I wanted to be one of them.

The only hard part is that I'm not sure I have that degree of coordination.

You have to be able to pat your head, chew gum, and write a novel, all at the same time.

Normally I can only do one of these at once.

Chew gum.

So I researched the customer reviews of the treadmill desks, and the idea started to grow on me. So the moral of the story is that sometimes things that look ridiculous might turn into a necessity, which is a moral I forgot when I saw elsewhere on the website that they actually sold desks attached to bicycles.

A cycling desk?

Now *that's* ridiculous.

I think.

HOT WHEELS

BY FRANCESCA

I'm not much of a driver. So imagine my surprise when I found myself behind the wheel of a Porsche 911 Carrera 4S.

But there I was, driving it at 70 mph an hour with the wind in my hair and four hundred horsepower in front of me.

Or is it behind me? Where's the engine on a Porsche, again? Sorry, I'm really not a car person.

Let me shift this story into reverse. Recently, I went to visit my best friend and her fiancé at their beach rental in Rhode Island. The first day there, my friend and I spent the morning on the beach while her fiancé worked at the house. When we got hungry, she said there was a great little seafood shack just a short drive away.

I was thrilled. I'd been dying to take a ride in the Porsche since her boyfriend got it six months ago. Not only was it a marvel for any of my friends to have a car in the city, but this was a too-die-for beautiful, *bona fide* sports car.

As Ferris Bueller once said, if you have the means, I highly recommend picking one up.

"Babe, can we take the car?" my friend called into the house from the porch.

"Sure," her fiancé answered, then added, "But only if Francesca drives."

Moi?

"Wait, why can't you drive it?" I said, offended on her behalf.

But she explained that her wallet was stolen and she hadn't gotten around to replacing her license, so she'd never driven the car. It still didn't explain why I was deemed trustworthy to drive it, but who am I to ask questions?

I took the keys like Gollum receiving Precious.

Just sitting in the driver's seat was fun. The inside of this car looked like a jet cockpit.

But I couldn't even find the ignition — "Uh, just give me a minute," I said — not exactly *Top Gun* material.

"Don't be nervous, we're just going to be driving ten minutes, nothing over 35 mph, and basically all one road. It's the easiest drive in the world."

When I finally got the engine running, I tapped the gas and lurched forward. My previous driving experience was all but exclusive to a 2002 Volkswagen Cabrio, a windup toy by comparison.

The Carrera needs to be caressed.

So I recalibrated my plebeian foot to one light as a ballet dancer, and we were on our way.

We got to the lunch spot, no problem. I parked about fifty yards from the nearest car, terrified of someone scratching or even sneezing on this gorgeous machine.

Especially since it wasn't *my* gorgeous machine.

When we were finished, we got back in the car, my friend said, "The gas tank is almost empty, let's do him a favor and fill it up before we go back."

"Is there a station nearby?" The community where we were staying was pretty remote.

"Google Maps on my phone says one is not far at all." She put the address in the car's GPS, and a woman began to direct me back onto the main road in soothing tones.

Even her voice sounded expensive.

We were going along, when the GPS directed me to take a right. "You know, this looks like an on-ramp. Do you still want me to take it?"

"It's not," my friend said, glued to her iPhone. "Turn here."

Thirty seconds later, we were on a major highway, where the 65 mph speed limit was treated by drivers as a suggestion, at best.

"I don't know what happened, I thought we were staying on the main road!" my friend cried.

Then the GPS had us get off at the next exit.

"See?" she said. "Phew, I knew it was a mistake."

Before it redirected us right back on the highway in the opposite direction, this time leading us to a huge bridge over the water.

"Omigod, are you okay?" she asked, sounding not-so-okay herself.

I didn't want her to panic, nor did I want to betray mine. I tried not to stammer. "I'm fine, we're perfectly safe, but I'm anxious just because, you know, it's not my car, and it's a very expensive car . . ."

"No kidding! It's a —"

She said how much the car cost, and it was double what I had guessed — my stomach dropped deeper into the bucket seat.

You know how they say, don't borrow

anything you can't afford to replace?

As I white-knuckled the wheel over the crest of the bridge, I envisioned the final scene in *Thelma and Louise*. Because if I damaged this car in any way, that seemed like my best option.

I'd say, "Let's not get caught. Let's keep goin.' "

She could get out first — her fiancé *loved* her — but I'd have to drive into the sky.

My only regret would be I didn't get a night with Brad Pitt first.

But the growl of six cylinders brought me back into the present. What was I afraid of? I had the power of the Porsche on my side. I put my foot on the gas and felt the car bite into the asphalt.

I started to have fun.

The hard part came later, when we needed to cross a lane of traffic in order to turn into the gas station. No one was letting us in, and I couldn't really blame them.

Two blondes in a Porsche don't exactly inspire sympathy and friendship.

I needed a bumper sticker that said, "my other car is the subway."

Cue the next round of bystander scorn as I had to approach the fueling station twice to get within reach of the gas tank, located in *front* of the passenger side.

I had checked that the parking brake was on three times before this photo was taken.

I mean, for such a nice car, you'd think they'd put the tank in the right place.

The return trip was easier. I even felt

comfortable enough to play music although I had my friend find the radio stations. I still wasn't taking my hands off ten and two.

When we safely pulled into the driveway, we were both giddy with relief. I walked into the beach house on jelly legs.

"Hey, you guys were gone a long time," her fiancé said. "I was almost worried."

"Oh no, everything was fine," my friend said. "And we filled up the tank for you."

"Aw, thanks." He kissed her on the cheek.

"Thanks for letting me drive it," I said in a small voice, handing back the keys as sheepish as a kid in the principal's office.

"Oh, anytime," he said.

I glanced at my friend.

She smiled.

THE SECOND-GREATEST GENERATION

BY LISA

I give my generation a lot of credit.

Somebody has to.

Why do I think credit is in order, in addition to my general mode of goodwill and self-congratulation?

Because I've been thinking about the enormous changes my generation has seen in its lifetime, and despite the fact that people generally don't like change, we've done remarkably well with it.

Take the changes in technology alone.

They say you should count your blessings, and I do. So let's take a moment to count our digital blessings.

On our digits.

For example, my generation will remember that televisions were black-and-white and had only four channels.

That happened.

We know.

We were there.

We remember the first time somebody on the street got a color television, which was invariably in somebody else's house. On my street, we actually stood outside their house, looking inside their picture window at the marvelous colors flickering on their faces in the darkness.

Okay, now flash forward to today.

When the TV has forty thousand channels, of course in color, plus movies and the like, and despite what people whine about, there's usually something pretty terrific on somewhere — and if you decide you have to go to the bathroom during the best part, you can stop the television.

Can you believe that?

Can you believe that you can actually *stop the television*?

I still don't even understand that.

I just take for granted that the planet has a rotational path as well as a gravitational pull, and so the very idea that I can alter, stop, or even reverse the forces of nature blows my tiny little mind.

Not only that, but I remember the TV days of yore, when you actually had to make a point of being in front of the television when the show came on.

Because the shows were on only at certain times.

And everybody had to watch the show at the same time.

We didn't determine the time the show was on, the networks did, and we built our lives around the show.

At least The Flying Scottolines did.

If you didn't, you would "miss the show."

What?

Nowadays, you never have to miss the show. You can watch the show whenever you want to. You can watch it over and over again.

Incredible!

All you have to do is learn how to work your remote.

We may not be The Greatest Generation, but at least we figured that out.

We're smarter than our remote controls.

Even if we didn't live through the Depression.

Call us the Second-Greatest Generation.

Take that, Tom Brokaw.

Let's not dwell on the fact that as cool as it was to tape TV shows, we never could figure out how to program our VCRs.

It doesn't matter. In the end, the VCRs died and we're still here.

Suck it, VCRs.

Payback's a bitch.

And then there are computers, which are

remarkable in every way, and without which I couldn't do my job. I'm constantly writing and editing, and I can do that with the click of a mouse, instead of the old days, when I remember cutting and pasting.

Do you remember having to type on a sheet, and then when you wanted to edit, physically getting a scissors, taping the line over the previous line, and Xeroxing it?

Or using Wite-out?

Which couldn't even spell its own name?

And there was something called carbon paper?

What the hell were we thinking?

And now the computers are so little we can hold them in our back pocket, and just the other day when I was walking the dogs, I was able to listen to one of two thousand songs, without even carrying a transistor radio.

Do you remember transistor radios?

And Walkman?

And Discman, which showed you were superwealthy because you had something called compact discs?

Shiny!

But now we have phones, which not only play music but take our picture, make movies of our lives, and even, remarkably, let us talk to one another whenever we want to, wherever we want to.

I know this sounds like Captain Obvious, but really, isn't that incredible?

By the way, you'll always sound like Captain Obvious when you count your blessings.

Care not.

Count anyway.

Meanwhile, while we're on the subject of phones, do you remember when you had to hang around the house, unable to go anywhere, waiting for a call from a doctor, or your mother, or your new crush?

That was then, this is better.

And paradoxically, sometimes the new technology is the old technology.

For example, the other day I was looking at my phone and discovered that it has a compass inside.

Well, not *inside*.

God knows where the compass is.

The same place the phone is.

The phone and the compass and the TV and the camera and the record player are the same thing.

And all I can tell you is that after I discovered that my phone was also a compass, I spent a good part of the afternoon walking northwest across my kitchen and trying to orient myself in the cosmos.

Until I realized that the cosmos was in my very hand.

It's the *greatest.*

And so are we.

CLIFF DIVING

BY FRANCESCA

If all your friends jumped off a cliff, would you do it?

Apparently, I would.

With my toes at the edge of a slippery rock thirty feet above the choppy sea, I realized that at twenty-eight years old, I'm still as susceptible to peer pressure as I was at sixteen.

I was spending the weekend with my best friend and her fiancé in Little Compton, Rhode Island, with a bunch of his friends, and on this particular afternoon, I'd let the boys talk me into going cliff diving.

A fun fact about me: I'm terrified of heights. I mean truly phobic, in that there is no reasoning behind my fear, I know it's stupid, but I have a physical reaction to feeling high up and precarious. My legs turn to Jell-O, my hands shake, my heart races, and I have the overwhelming urge to crouch and crawl — anything to get closer to sea level.

And now I found myself literally looking down at the ocean.

Let me rewind fifteen minutes, to when I was happily, safely lounging on the beach now a hundred yards out of reach. My bestie and I were sunning ourselves on this glorious day, picking out all the most horrible gowns from the stack of bridal magazines we'd brought.

We were debating whether or not ribbon belts are figure-flattering or hopelessly played-out when her fiancé and his handsome British friend found our beach towel.

"It's that time of the day!" her fiancé cried. "We're going to the cliff!"

"Huh?" I said, squinting up at them.

He pointed out to the ocean, to where people the size of specks were lined up and throwing themselves off a tall, rocky outpost and into the sea, like lemmings. "It's really fun, the best part of my day."

"Yes, Francesca, you have to jump with us," added the Brit. The only thing I liked about the sentence was my name in his brogue.

"Oh-kay. I'll go," I said, getting up slowly.

"Have fun," my friend chirped.

"Aren't you coming?" I asked.

"Absolutely not," she answered.

I looked back at the guys, as if to say, wait,

"no" was an option?

"I'll watch," she said, without lifting her eyes from the magazine.

I instantly regretted my hasty agreement. But I wanted to seem like a fun gal, up for anything. Maybe my fear of heights had diminished with age, I thought.

Wishful thinking.

I swam out to the cliff with the guys, my dread growing with every stroke. When we reached the rock face, a lifeguard posted on the cliff — yes, before you get too impressed, this cliff was so "rugged" it had a lifeguard — called down to us as we bobbed in the choppy water.

"Sorry guys, you just missed the last jump. Tide is too low, you'll have to come out later."

Welp, too bad, let's swim back.

"Aw, can't we go real fast?" pleaded the fiancé.

"All right, be fast."

The Brit beamed. "Great! Thanks, mate!"

Yes. Thanks.

The guys quickly scrambled up the ladder nailed into the side of the rock, while I struggled to grasp the slippery, algae-covered rungs.

But I couldn't wimp out now. What would they think of me? I sucked in my breath and climbed up.

My legs were so shaky, I could barely lift my leg over the top rung and onto the rock, but I did it. There were ledges of graduated heights, and, of course, the boys had to climb to the very highest one.

I followed just so I didn't have to be alone.

I decided I had to go second if I was going to go at all. The Brit went first, and the fiancé agreed to stay behind for moral support.

While I stood trying to screw up my courage, below me an attractive, shirtless man with an accent was beckoning me — in most circumstances, any one of those traits would do the trick, but, at the moment, I was numb. The only thing that was going to get me to jump was the knowledge that only jumping would get me off this miserable rock face with the wind whipping across my body.

If I didn't jump soon, I was likely to faint.

So I counted to three and leapt. I held my breath and my nose, but the cliff was so high, I nearly ran out of breath before I hit the water.

The impact gave me an atomic wedgie worthy of the Bikini Atoll.

Check back in nine months, I may give birth to a fish.

The cliff at its most welcoming

But I survived, my top stayed on, and I was back at sea level — I was elated. The boys congratulated me for my courage. Apparently I'm a better actress than I thought.

"Thank you, thank you," I said. "You know, it wasn't so bad. If the lifeguard had let us, I would've gone a second time," I lied.

"Let's ask!"

Damnit.

So I jumped off the cliff twice that day.

And I hated it both times.

As the weekend progressed, more and

more of the fiancé's friends arrived, most of whom I had never met before. I did have my best friend there, but she was often busy playing hostess with her hubby-to-be, or I imagined they were trying to get some rare alone time, and I didn't want to seem clingy. The new people were all friendly and cool, but they were old college chums with an easy comfort. I tried to be my most "on" to win them over, but I still often felt a beat behind. I hadn't been so desperate to be liked since I switched districts in sixth grade.

What does it feel like to be the new kid when you're almost thirty?

The same.

So I continued to go with the flow, even if doing so required me to swim upstream. When we all got stir-crazy one Saturday night, someone suggested a drinking game, but the only liquor we had extra of?

Warm red wine.

And another fun fact about me? I'm not very good at drinking games.

So I got more sloshed than I have in years. While several other girls demurred, I was easily goaded into being the last woman standing.

Later, one of the guys who works for an e-cigarette company produced samples of the product. I have never smoked a regular cigarette, or anything else, in my life, not even the lone joint in college. And although I don't have the same heath aversion to e-cigarettes, they've always struck me as kind of douchey.

And yet that night, I declined only once before caving. Soon I was puffing away on an e-cig, feeling like a complete idiot, but a popular one.

But, Mom, everyone was doing it.

The next day, thanks to chugging red wine and sucking enough nicotine vapor to keep Kate Moss buzzed, I had one of the worst hangovers of my life. And somewhere between the headaches and the dizzy spells, I thought, what the hell am I doing?

They say, if I knew then what I know now . . .

My motto of the weekend should've been, if I knew now what I used to know then.

In high school I was actually more im-mune to peer pressure and truer to myself than I had been that weekend. Because back then, I was in my comfort zone. I grew up there, I knew everyone, and I went home every day to my mom. I wanted for noth-ing.

It's easy to jump with a safety net.

Now, I live alone in the city, and I'm performing the high-wire act of every twenty-something who's trying to balance career goals with personal ones, not to mention a checkbook. I struggle to walk the line of building the person I want to be while only being the person I am.

And after ending a two-year relationship, I had to say goodbye to the entire network of my ex-boyfriend's friends, many of whom I'd grown close to. Now I have to create a new network, from scratch.

So I admit, I wanted these people to like me. I wanted to be in their group.

And I want my novel to get published this year. And I want to meet a wonderful man. And I want to be happy.

I want everything.

But when the pounding in my temples subsided, I knew I'd have to be myself to get it.

The next day was my last in Little Compton. I thought my girlfriend would be able to drive me to the train station an hour away, but I forgot she didn't have a valid license, so the Brit gallantly offered to give me a lift.

During the drive, we got to talking on a deeper level than we had all weekend. And again, I found myself out of my comfort zone. But this time, I spoke with uncalculated honesty.

Without meaning to, I found myself telling him my life's story. My "dynamic" family history of divorce, remarriage, and divorce, my own thoughts about marriage and kids.

As far as having romantic "game" goes, this was as un-strategic as it gets. The TMI factor was giving me anxiety, but despite my better judgment, I couldn't stop my mouth.

I think, on some level, I wanted him to know me before I left.

The me who's afraid of heights, and a lightweight, and a little square, and not very well traveled. The real me.

We're getting drinks next week.

One, two, three, jump.

DOES THIS BEACH MAKE ME LOOK OLD?

BY LISA

I joke about getting older, but the truth is, I don't feel old.

On the contrary, at age fifty-nine, I feel as if I'm entering my prime.

So I'm either delusional or insightful.

I'll leave the choice to you.

But let me make my case.

I'll begin not by talking about myself, but about my girlfriends, all of whom are my age. We've been friends for many years. And when I look at the things they're doing, I realize they're in their prime too. In fact they're more primy than I am.

My friend Franca runs every day and lifts weights, and she's about to run her first marathon.

I'm going with her, to cheer.

That's how I work out, by cheering.

My friend Paula is going on a trip to New Zealand with her husband and is planning on hiking twenty miles. She hikes every day here at home and has hiked the Grand Tetons in Wyoming.

They're Grand!

And my friend Nan trains horses and can ride anything with four legs.

Not bad for the Middle Ages, are they?

They aren't what I thought the fifties would look like when I was growing up, and I don't think it's just that my perception has changed because I'm in my fifties.

I think the fifties have changed. Since the way we saw them, back in the fifties.

And it's not just physical activity. In fact, we're better in many other ways. Paula travels the world, Nan rehabs houses, and Franca donates her time to help children with special needs.

We're trying new things.

Wonder why?

I think we women spend so much of our lives taking care of other people that when the kids grow up, we come to realize that it's time to truly take care of ourselves, and once we make that decision, our lives change.

More accurately, we change our lives.

I'll speak for myself, because I know I have, but it's been part of an evolution. For example, writing is my favorite thing in the world, and I think I'm getting better at it, but it's taken me twenty years of practice and twenty-odd novels to date. So I've decided to write two novels a year instead of one, in addition to these memoirs.

Fun!

And to make this happen, I've changed the way I spend my day, prioritizing writing and saying no to things that interfere with my writing time.

In the beginning, I felt guilty when I said no, aware that I was disappointing people.

But then a miracle happened.

I got used to it.

And it got easier.

I stopped giving away my time. Instead I'm giving myself permission to keep it and use it the way I want.

So I don't meet people I don't want to see for lunch.

I don't talk on the phone with anyone when I don't want to.

I don't impose obligations on myself, or allow others to impose them on me.

It's taken me almost six decades on earth to figure this out, but here I am.

And in my free time when I'm not writing, I do only the things I want to do, like see friends, read, walk the dogs, and ride bikes or Buddy The Pony.

I'm happier than I've ever been.

I've come into myself.
Every woman does.
We find out who we really are.
We grow.
And in that way, we never grow old.

ACKNOWLEDGMENTS
BY LISA AND FRANCESCA

We would like to express our love and gratitude to St. Martin's Press for supporting this book and its predecessors. First, thanks to Coach Jen Enderlin, our terrific editor, as well as to the brilliant John Sargent, Sally Richardson, Jeff Dodes, Jeff Capshew, Stephanie Davis, Brian Heller, Jen Gonzalez, Paul Hochman, Jeanne-Marie Hudson, John Karle, Tracey Guest, Michael Storrings, Anne-Marie Tallberg, Nancy Trypuc, Caitlin Dareff, and all the amazing sales reps. We appreciate so much your enthusiasm for these books, and we thank you for everything you do to support us. And we will always love and remember the late Matthew Shear, whom we adored.

We'd also like to thank Mary Beth Roche, Laura Wilson, Esther Bochner, Brant Janeway, and the St. Martin's audiobook division for giving us the opportunity to record our own audiobook of this volume and the others in the series. We love to do it, and we love audiobooks! And there is simply no substitute for our Philly accents, which come free of charge!

Huge thanks and love to our amazing agents, Molly Friedrich, Lucy Carson, and Nicole Lefebvre of the Friedrich Agency. Thanks to *The Philadelphia Inquirer,* which carries our "Chick Wit" column, and to our editor, the wonderful Sandy Clark.

One of the best people in the world is Laura Leonard, and her advice, friendship, and love sustain us. Laura, thank you so much for all of your great comments and suggestions on this manuscript. We owe you, forever.

Love to our girlfriends! Lisa would like to thank Nan Daley, Paula Menghetti, Sandy Steingard, and Franca Palumbo. Francesca would like to thank Rebecca Harrington, Katy Andersen, Courtney Yip, Janie Stolar, Megan Amram, and right-hand-man, Ryder Kessler. Thank you for being there during a difficult year. We're blessed in all of you.

Family is the heart of this book, because family is the heart of everything. Special thanks and love to Brother Frank.

We miss Mother Mary and the late Frank Scottoline terribly, but they are with us always.

Finally, thank you to our readers. Now, you're family.

ABOUT THE AUTHORS

Lisa Scottoline is a *New York Times* bestselling and Edgar Award–winning author of twenty-four novels and coauthor of six humor memoirs in this series. She also writes a Sunday column for *The Philadelphia Inquirer*. She has 30 million copies of her books in print, and she has been published in thirty countries. She lives in the Philadelphia suburbs with an array of disobedient pets. You can visit Lisa at scottoline.com.

Francesca Serritella is the coauthor of six humor memoirs in this series and is currently working on a novel. She is also a Sunday columnist for *The Philadelphia Inquirer*. Francesca is a cum laude and award-winning graduate of Harvard University and now lives in New York City with one dog and one cat, so far. You can visit Francesca at francescaserritella.com.